STAYING SOBER

A GUIDE FOR RELAPSE PREVENTION

STAYING SOBER

A GUIDE FOR RELAPSE PREVENTION

Terence T. Gorski and Merlene Miller

Foreword by Father Martin

Based on the Gorski-CENAPS® Model

Herald House/Independence Press
1001 West Walnut
P.O. Box 390
Independence, Missouri 64051-0390
1-800-767-8181
(816) 521-3015

ISBN 978-0-8309-0459-4
Printed in the United States of America

Dedication

This book is dedicated to Richard Weedman, a mentor who saw potential that no one else could see and conjured up the magic of inspiration that made this book and so much more possible.

Acknowledgments

It is impossible to list all of the people who have contributed to the development of the relapse prevention planning concepts that are described in this book. We have attempted to identify those who have most strongly contributed.

Special acknowledgments go to Richard D. Weedman, currently a national consultant for the National Association of Alcoholism Treatment Programs and to the late Stan Martindale who was Professor of Psychology at Northeastern Illinois University. It was through five years of initial training with Richard Weedman that the foundation concepts of relapse prevention planning came into being. Stan's indepth training in Gestalt and Humanistic Psychology allowed the marriage of these concepts with the current efforts in relapse prevention planning. Jim Kelleher, as supervisor and good friend, encouraged the development of the 37 warning signs.

We would like to thank Dr. James Milam, the Executive Director of the Milam Recovery Center, whose pioneering work in the disease concept of alcoholism and its neurological effects has greatly influenced the development of our concepts. He has been extremely helpful through hours of conversation regarding the material presented here.

Dr. Henri Begleiter, Professor of Psychiatry and Neuroscience at State University of New York College of Medicine was very helpful in validating that relapse theory and relapse prevention planning methods are on good scientific ground. G. Douglas Talbott, M.D. helped review the manuscript. His work in understanding the physiological basis of the disease of alcoholism was instrumental in relating the post acute withdrawal symptomatology with the relapse concepts.

In the past six years over three hundred training and treatment organizations have sponsored training in relapse prevention. The people who had the foresight and courage to explore this newly developed area were directly responsible for its growth and development. Although these individuals are too numerous to reference, several require special mention.

The alcoholism treatment centers at Illinois Central Community Hospital (now Hyde Park Community Hospital) in Chicago, and Ingalls Memorial Hospital in Harvey, Illinois, were responsible for primary clinical applications of this model between 1974 and 1982. Through the efforts of Hal Thompson, Bob Edwards, and Ann Miller, the Loala Center in Lebanon, Indiana, was the first to implement a comprehensive relapse prevention tract based on this model in 1984.

In 1986 Father Martin's Ashley opened a comprehensive relapse prevention center. Father Martin, Lora Mae and Thomas Abraham, Micki Thomas, and most recently, Robert Shelton provided valuable assistance in implementing these new methods and giving us feedback. It has been an honor to work with Father Martin. His vision and support provided tremendous encouragement. Through his efforts Ashley took a pioneering step in opening a specialty relapse prevention program that integrates spirituality with relapse prevention methods.

John Harnish of St. John and West Shore Hospital in Westlake, Ohio; Tom Hedin, the State Director for the Division of Alcohol and Substance Abuse in North Dakota; Dan Barmettler of the Institute for Integral Development; Jim Porter, Executive Director of the Mile High Council on Alcoholism in Denver; Lisa Havens, the Director of Maplewood Center of Howard Community Hospital in Kokomo, Indiana; and Marjorie Kimmel, the Executive Director of First City Recovery Center in Ohio have also been strong supporters of these concepts in their areas.

Dick Jeske, a trainer for the Department of the Navy, has provided assistance in helping to reconcile the Relapse Prevention self-help groups with the principles of Alcoholics Anonymous and related self-help groups. Tammy Bell, EAP Administrator for Borg-Warner Chemicals, Inc. has been instrumental in relating these concepts to alcoholics in the work place.

We would like to thank Claudia Black for her detailed review of this manuscript and the discussions about the relationship of relapse to adult children of alcoholics. Although a great deal of the information is not present in this current volume, these conversations and comments helped shape our thinking and will be reflected in future works.

The work of Stephanie Brown, Ph.D., consultant to

Stanford Alcohol Clinic, in the developmental model of recovery and her careful and critical review of the manuscript was helpful in clarifying the theoretical basis of these concepts.

Tom Claunch and Frank Lisnow, past president and president, respectively, of the National Association of Alcoholism and Drug Abuse Counselors (NAADAC) also have our thanks for reviewing this manuscript and submitting comments.

Thanks to others who reviewed this manuscript: Al Grossenbacher for reviewing it from the perspective of AA principles; Gary G. Forrest of Psychotherapy Associates in Colorado Springs; Maxwell N. Weisman, M.D., Baltimore, Maryland; and G. Alan Marlatt, Director of Addictive Behaviors Research Center, University of Washington, Seattle, Washington.

Joe Troiani, the Program Director of the Alcohol Education Center of Loretto Hospital in Chicago, has provided hours of support and encouragement in this project. His patience and willingness to act as a sounding board is greatly appreciated.

Thanks to Russell Gilbreth, Kathy Chidichimo, Mary Johnson, and Susan Hall who provided assistance in the typing and development of the numerous manuscript drafts. A special thanks to Anne Dickerson, Jean Hurshman, Ann Welch, Tim Markwell, Jan Hankins, Lori Roberts, and Cleona Guthrie for proofreading and for reading and rereading manuscripts and providing feedback.

We can never put into words our appreciation to Jan Smith and David Miller, our spouses, who have given so much to make this book possible. In addition to hours of time, they have given us love, support, encouragement, and a lot of hand holding.

The most important people to thank are the recovering alcoholics themselves. They struggle with their recovery daily and periodically relapse because of our limited understanding of their disease and how to treat it. It is through their suffering, courage, strength, and hope that relapse prevention planning has been possible.

Table of Contents

Foreword

We are all well aware of the basic destructive nature of the disease of alcoholism. It affects its human victim in body, mind, emotion, and soul. Of its nature, it is terminal. We know it cannot be cured, but it can be arrested. Many hundreds of thousands of alcoholics over the past 50 years have arrested their disease and lived happy, effective and productive, sober lives. One of the great tragedies, however, in this field is the fact that many alcoholics get well for a time and then return to drinking.

It is said that approximately half of the alcoholics, who come to the door of sobriety, enter and stay. Of the remaining alcoholics, many stay for a time and have one or more relapses and then grasp the sober life and stay sober until death. Of the remaining alcoholics, many go through what we call the revolving door, over and over again, being sober and then returning to drinking. Some of these, of course, eventually die.

Terry Gorski, early in his professional career, was assigned to try to help these "end of the roaders." He felt that some of them obviously were completely incapable of getting well; the damage done them by their drinking was too great to be repaired. Of the rest, however, he felt that it should be possible to help them get the sobriety that others had grasped a little more easily than they. And so this young man spent fifteen years of his life (and is still working at it) studying case history after case history numbering in the thousands of these poor unfortunates who return time and time again to drinking.

Out of it all came his CENAPS model of relapse prevention. It integrates Alcoholics Anonymous with professional treatment and creates a road map or guide to recovery. As he said, this guide is nothing new of and by itself. What it does is integrate the wisdom of the AA recovery program with all the research of the past few decades.

I believe in the concepts that are described in the manual. So strong is my belief in their effectiveness that we are implementing a comprehensive relapse prevention center at Ashley. It will provide the finest integration of professional counseling, medical treatment and the wisdom of Alcoholics Anonymous.

I believe that this book and its accompanying relapse prevention workbook can provide you with valuable information that may save your life. If in attempting to understand and apply this information you find you cannot do it alone, do not give up hope. There are many fine treatment centers that can help you with relapse prevention planning.

No matter what is done, however, some folks will die of this terminal illness. However, too many will still continue to die because we do not understand how to treat the phenomenon of relapse. Relapse prevention planning is a powerful new approach that is helping thousands to escape from what had previously been a death sentence. It is important that we convey the message to relapse-prone alcoholics that there really is hope. It is time that we convey the message to treatment centers that we have a moral obligation to give our best efforts to heal the sickest of the sick among the ranks of alcoholics. I believe that this book opens an excellent way to begin to help people who were previously considered hopeless.

Father Joseph C. Martin
Cofounder
Father Martin's Ashley
Havre de Grace, Maryland

Preface

In the early 1970s I was working as an alcoholism counselor at Grant Hospital in Chicago. Starting in June of 1971 I was assigned to full time responsibility in the outpatient department. Because I had low seniority in the agency, I had very little influence in getting assigned "high prognosis patients." I was assigned the most difficult patients, many of them having had treatment numerous time without attaining sobriety. At that time I was not concerned. I believed I could work with anybody. Nobody ever told me that these chronic relapse prone patients were hopeless. As a result I simply expected them to recover.

When a caseload is exclusively composed of relapse prone individuals it can be an overwhelming task, but I began learning almost immediately.

The first thing that I learned was that most relapse prone patients had experienced everything that alcoholism counseling and traditional psychotherapy had to offer. I also learned that many had more knowledge of the steps and traditions of A.A. than I did. They knew the "Big Book" and the "Twelve and Twelve." Many had long periods of abstinence that were achieved by practicing the A.A. principles. But somehow they could not put those principles to work in their lives. Many felt that they were constitutionally "incapable of recovery" and related to the statement in Chapter 5 of the "Big Book" that describes those unfortunates who cannot recover.

I had been trained in a highly confrontive style of therapy. I quickly learned that confrontation would not work with relapse prone patients because the one thing they had more experience with than anything else was dealing with confrontive people. On a day-to-day basis they were confronted by almost everyone—employers, wives, children, therapists, counselors, police officers, etc. If there was one thing they were skilled at it was dealing with confrontation.

I quickly recognized that this group of patients was harder on themselves than any therapist could ever be. They tended to punish themselves and put themselves down. Their self-esteem was at an all-time low.

During the first several months of attempting to work with these patients I experienced very little success. I decided to forget about traditional alcoholism counseling and begin to learn from the true experts, the patients themselves.

Instead of launching into sophisticated treatment plans, highly confrontational treatment strategies, and highly structured treatment programs I adopted a much simpler approach. First, I asked each patient to attend a minimum of three AA meetings per week.

Second, I devised a special three-hour therapy group that helped the people learn how to communicate with one another, how to experience and talk about feelings and emotions, and how to identify general patterns of behavior in the group and then apply these patterns to problems occurring in other areas of their lives.

The third part of the treatment consisted of individual therapy sessions which were devoted almost exclusively to constructing a detailed relapse history. They were encouraged to start with the last time that they started a period of sobriety. I was surprised to find that most were convinced they were alcoholic and needed an on-going recovery program prior to their most recent relapse. I was also surprised to find that most of these people were highly motivated to stay sober. They did not want to relapse. They were willing to use Alcoholics Anonymous (AA), professional counseling, and just about anything else a treatment program would recommend. Some had experienced electric shock therapy or aversive conditioning (where they were forced to vomit when they drank). Others were voluntarily locked away for periods of months. Most got drunk again in spite of these extensive efforts.

My goal in collecting these relapse histories was to assemble a detailed step-by-step accounting as to how someone committed to sobriety and knowledgable about alcoholism could return to drinking. How could alcoholics convince themselves to take a drink that they knew would probably kill them?

What I learned from collecting these relapse histories was that there were many similarities among patients. It seemed that most people followed the same patterns of thinking, emotional reactions, behaviors, and life situations that led to relapse.

After taking five or six histories I discovered how difficult it was for these recovering alcoholics to sort out their thoughts and their feelings. It became apparent that they were not able to think clearly, process their feelings and emotions or even remember things. Their ability to deal with abstractions and reconstruct their history was extremely limited. The first several histories took as long as six to ten hours to complete. People had large gaps in memory, large periods of time that they did not remember. They also had a great deal of difficulty assembling past events in logical sequential order. When I asked them to describe what certain past activities or actions meant they were incapable of assigning meaning to them. They could deal with concrete recollections, but they had great difficulty abstracting and generalizing the meaning of those experiences to other life situations.

After completing approximately ten histories, I compared the results. I took the similarities and began constructing a common list of what I called relapse warning signs. Instead of starting from scratch in history taking with a new patient I would show a new patient this list of warning signs. At this time the warning signs were a simple listing of words and short phrases such as denial, defensive behavior, crisis building, and so forth. I would explain what each of these meant in an individual therapy session and use this to prod their memory to see if they had experienced these things.

I found that by using this list I could greatly speed up the history taking process. I also found that in the therapy group more and more patients were volunteering to talk about their relapse warning signs. Many also began to see patterns that led to drinking in the past. They began recognizing these same warning signs as they began to occur in their current sobriety.

The focus of the group rapidly changed from a psychologically oriented growth group to a very concrete relapse prevention oriented therapy group. The focus was on identifying concrete warning signs of relapse, recognizing them in real-life situations and learning how to take concrete steps to reverse the warning signs.

Although I did not know it at the time, this three-hour group therapy coupled with this individual relapse history process and continued involvement in AA became the foundation of a comprehensive relapse theory and practice that became known as Relapse Prevention Planning.

Over the course of two years as an outpatient therapist I collected 118 relapse histories and I set to the task of analyzing in detail these relapse histories. The end result of this was a revised list of 37 warning signs that were supported by the general patterns that were evident in these 118 histories.

In June of 1973 I left Grant Hospital to begin working as an EAP Program Coordinator for the Department of the Army in Fort Sheridan, Illinois. More work was accomplished in the area of relapse prevention. In August of 1974 I became the Director of The Department of Alcoholism Services at Illinois Central Community Hospital, now Hyde Park Community Hospital in Chicago,

Illinois. The work in this program further confirmed the relapse dynamic.

In 1976 I became the Director of the Alcoholism Treatment Center at Ingalls Memorial Hospital in Harvey, Illinois. I began working extensively with Dr. Harry Hannig, M.D. Together we worked with patients who were relapse prone. We had a traditional alcoholism rehabilitation center, but we very rapidly recognized the need to provide specialty services for relapse prone patients.

All staff members were trained in the basic principles of relapse prevention. We identified the counterproductive attitudes and mistaken beliefs that increased the relapse problem. We also reevaluated our policy of harsh confrontation, and we began to separate patients who were simply not motivated to comply with treatment from those who were willing to comply but for whom traditional treatment didn't work.

We found that after relapse prevention therapy these patients had fewer relapses and experienced longer periods of sobriety. If they did return to alcohol and drug use, their relapses tended to be shorter and the severity of consequences tended to be less than those who were treated with other methods. We were hopeful and excited.

In 1979 I affiliated with Merlene Miller. Merlene was a professional educator and writer. Together we began organizing the material that would act as the foundation of a new model of counseling based primarily upon relapse prevention technologies. Our initial organization was called Alcoholism Systems Associates (ASA) and operated out of Hazelcrest, Illinois. We did local training in the Chicago area and slowly a national reputation for these methods began to build.

In 1982 we published a book entitled ***Counseling for Relapse Prevention,*** which made explicit for the first time the basic principles and strategies of relapse prevention planning. The first half of the book was devoted to relapse theory, and the second half to describing the practical steps of relapse prevention. This book was written to counselors, but many recovering people began to use it in their own recovery.

In the early 1980s we became aware of the work of G. Alan Marlatt and his associates at Addictive Behaviors Research Center, University of Washington in Seattle. Although his work comes from a behaviorist school rather than a disease concept school of thought, the actual treatment procedures for preventing relapse are remarkably similar. The Behaviorist School has contributed a wealth of research confirming the effectiveness of relapse prevention planning. In 1985 the book, *Relapse Prevention,* edited by G. Alan Marlatt and Judith R. Gordon, gathered together for the first time a summary and integration of that empirical research.

This current book, ***Staying Sober—A Guide to Relapse Prevention,*** is an effort to update the relapse prevention model with the new information that has been learned since our previous book. It is also an effort to bring directly to you, members of the recovering community, vital information that can make the difference between life and death—between sobriety and relapse.

It is the hope of Merlene and myself that the information in this book can allow you to share from the cumulative experiences of many thousands of alcoholics who have directly and indirectly contributed to the development of this model.

The book is presented to you in an effort to share our experiences and hopes with you. We want you to find hope. In that spirit let us begin a journey with you. A journey that will summarize in these pages the essential knowledge of relapse prevention that has taken us over fifteen years to assemble.

Terence T. Gorski

RECOMMENDED FOR CLINICAL USE WITH THIS BOOK

STAYING SOBER WORKBOOK

Staying Sober Workbook is designed to be used with *Staying Sober: A Guide for Relapse Prevention.* The step-by-step approach used in the workbook will be most helpful to persons in individual or group counseling sessions who are not recovering from chemical dependency.

Readers will be guided in examining the entire relapse process to better understand why they relapse and how they can prevent relapse from occurring. This method has been proven successful among many recovering alcoholics and those with chemical dependencies. These proven principles of relapse prevention planning, based on the CENAPS® Model of treatment, are presented in an understandable, workable way.

Chapter I

RELAPSE IN ADDICTIVE DISEASE

This is a book about relapse—what it is and, more importantly, how it can be prevented. The book is intended to comfort the disturbed and to disturb the comfortable. It will comfort the disturbed because many relapsed persons are victims of mistaken beliefs and have relapsed because they do not know how to prevent it. They blame themselves for past relapses and believe they are hopeless because they do not know what to do to prevent future relapse. It is our intent to give them hope, to correct their mistaken beliefs, and to help them set up plans based on accurate information that can free them from the hopelessness of repeated relapse.

We do not intend to disturb those who are comfortable in a healthy sobriety, but it is our intent to disturb the naively comfortable. These are the people who believe that as long as they abstain from alcohol and drugs and "bring the body" to meetings they do not need to be concerned about relapse. They are not aware that recovery is more than that. They are not aware that there are many, many individuals who are attending meetings and not drinking but who are still not sober. They are just not drinking or using drugs. These people are in high risk of relapse even though most of them will strongly deny that fact. We intend to show that realistically facing the possibility of relapse is the only way to prevent it.

Relapse is a complex process. It cannot be explained simply. There are many aspects of it that need to be understood. You may need to read this book more than once in order to really understand and apply the principles that we are attempting to explain. Since everything is so important, it has been difficult for us to choose what to deal with first. Maybe it will be helpful if we tell you now what to expect as you read this book.

First, we are going to discuss addictive disease. It is impossible to understand the process of relapse without understanding the condition to which one is relapsing.

Relapse is a problem that applies to a variety of addictions. A person may be addicted to alcohol or to other mood-altering drugs. Although much of the research into relapse was conducted with alcoholics (persons addicted to the drug alcohol) there is growing evidence that the same relapse prevention methods can be used with a variety of addictions. As a result, for the purpose of this book, we will use the following terms interchangeably: alcoholism, chemical dependence, addiction, and addictive disease. We will also use the terms alcoholic, chemically dependent person, addict, and addicted person to mean the same thing.

This book is written for persons recovering from addiction and will address you if you are one of those people. We believe, however, that it will be helpful to those who are not or have not been addicted, especially counselors and family members.

We will discuss addiction as a bio-psycho-social

disease. This means that it is a physical disease (bio) that also affects the mind (psycho) and relationships (social).

It has long been known that people with an addictive disease experience abnormal reactions not only to the use of the addictive chemical but to NOT using the chemical. When most people think about addictive disease they think only of the symptoms that occur while someone is actively involved in the addiction. They are not aware that there are symptoms that emerge with abstinence. These sobriety-based symptoms can be reactivated at any time during recovery. We are going to describe some of these symptoms in detail in the chapter on post acute withdrawal. Then we will describe management techniques that will help you lower the risk of experiencing post acute withdrawal.

To understand and prevent relapse it is also necessary to understand the recovery process and what happens when recovery is incomplete. We call this partial recovery. We are going to describe the normal process of recovery and take a look at what sometimes happens to block complete recovery from occurring.

There are mistaken beliefs about relapse that we will explore with you. These beliefs can increase the risk that relapse will occur. Changing some of those beliefs will allow you to change behaviors that lead to relapse.

Most people think of using addictive chemicals when they think of "relapse." Certainly addictive use is relapse. But because of research in recent years, more and more people are coming to recognize that the process of relapse begins before addictive use starts. People can become dysfunctional in sobriety without drinking or using. They can lose control of judgment and behavior. They can develop emotional problems or physical problems. They may become dysfunctional in sobriety ***before*** they begin addictive use or ***instead*** of addictive use.

The process of relapse goes beyond the traditional idea of relapse as alcohol or drug use to the understanding that the relapse process includes attitudes and behaviors that lead to active addictive using.

The relapse process is the movement away from recovery. This does not mean that if you have hit a rough spot in recovery or you are experiencing some pain and struggle in recovery that you are relapsing. It means that if, in general, you are not doing things that contribute to the process of recovery, you may be unconsciously moving in the direction of relapse. If you are stuck in partial recovery, you are in high risk of relapse.

Recovery from addictive disease starts with accepting the fact that you cannot safely use alcohol or mood-altering drugs. But just knowing that addictive chemicals are harmful is not enough. You must stop using them. Not using addictive chemicals is abstinence. But abstinence alone is not enough. Abstinence simply allows the recovery process to begin. It is the means to an end—the means to normal living. Learning to live normally without addictive use requires more than abstinence.

It is necessary to correct the physical, psychological,

and social damage to health caused by the addiction. It is also necessary to learn to live a healthy and productive life without the need for alcohol or other drugs or addictive behavior. The addicted person must learn to cope with life in a non-addictive manner.

Relapse and recovery are intimately related. You cannot experience recovery from addiction without experiencing a tendency toward relapse. Relapse tendencies are a normal and natural part of the recovery process. They are nothing to be ashamed of. They need to be dealt with openly and honestly. If they are not, they grow stronger. Relapse tendencies are a lot like poison mushrooms or mold. They grow best in the darkness. The light of clear accurate thinking tends to kill relapse tendencies very quickly.

When the sobriety-based symptoms of addiction become severe enough a person begins to become dysfunctional even though not drinking or using. In AA these episodes of dysfunction are known as "dry drunks." In this book we call them the relapse syndrome. When these symptoms of the relapse syndrome make life painful enough, many alcoholics choose to drink or use drugs to gain temporary relief from the pain. Others do not drink, but they develop serious life and health problems related to the relapse syndrome.

It is possible to interrupt the relapse syndrome before serious consequences occur by bringing the warning signs of relapse that you are experiencing into conscious awareness. This is relapse prevention planning. In the final part of this book we are going to explain relapse prevention planning. There is also a workbook available to guide you through the relapse prevention planning process and to help you develop a relapse prevention plan of your own.

Chapter II

ADDICTIVE DISEASE

In order to understand relapse, it is necessary to understand addictive disease. People often fail to recover because they do not understand their addiction or they fail to do those things that could help them to avoid relapse. Erroneous information about the nature of addiction is responsible for much improper and incomplete treatment that leads to relapse.

ADDICTIVE CHEMICALS

Mood-altering drugs are chemicals agents that produce changes in brain function by altering the chemistry of the brain. Once brain function is altered a person experiences physical, psychological, and behavioral changes as a direct result. These changes in physical and psychological functioning and in behavior cause changes in social relationships. All mood-altering drugs have the potential to alter thinking, to damage the mind, to damage the body and to affect behavior and relationships ***whether or not they are used addictively.*** The extent to which these consequences may occur depends upon the drug used, the person using the drug, and in some cases, the circumstances under which the drug is used.

The major addictive drugs can be classified in four groups. They are downers (depressants), uppers (stimulants), pain killers (narcotics), and mind benders (hallucinogenics). The drugs typically found under each of these categories are listed below.

1. ***DOWNERS***
   A. Alcohol
   B. Sleeping Pills (barbiturates and similar acting sedative hypnotics)
   C. Minor tranquilizers (Librium, Valium, etc.)

2. ***UPPERS***
   A. Amphetamines
   B. Cocaine
   C. Nicotine (tobacco)
   D. Caffeine

3. ***PAIN KILLERS***
   A. Narcotics
   B. Narcotic Derivatives

4. ***MIND BENDERS* (PERCEPTION DISTORTERS)**
   A. Hallucinogens
   B. Phenyclidine (PCP)
   C. Cannabis (Marijuana, Hashish, etc.)

THE DISEASE OF ADDICTION

"Addiction" is a condition in which a person develops bio-psycho-social dependence on any moodaltering substance. An addiction causes a person to use a drug for short-term gratification. But there is a price to be paid. The addiction creates long-term pain and discomfort. An addiction is accompanied by obsession, compulsion, and loss of control. When not using, the person who suffers an addiction thinks about, plans, and looks forward to using again. This is the obsession. Using interferes with living, but there is a compulsion or overwhelming urge to use again in spite of long-term painful consequences. The addicted person uses the drug to relieve the pain created by using the drug. Thus continued use of the chemical leads to continued use of the chemical. This is addiction.

Continued use of addictive chemicals leads to continued use of addictive chemicals.

Addiction is distinguished from drug use by the lack of freedom of choice. Using a mood-altering substance is a choice. Addiction is a condition that robs a person of choice and dictates the frequency, the quantity, and the nature of use. All addiction begins with use, but all use does not lead to addiction.

Addiction is a physical disease. It is properly classified with cancer, heart disease, and diabetes as a chronic illness that produces long-term physical, psychological, and social damage. Like victims of these other diseases, alcoholics have physical conditions that have caused them to be susceptible to developing the disease.

While alcoholism is widely accepted as a disease today, until very recent years it was considered a psychological or a moral issue. The work of Dr. E. M. Jelinek (17) in the '50s and '60s led to the acceptance of alcoholism as a disease by the American Medical Association (AMA), the American Medical Society on Alcoholism (AMSA), the National Council on Alcoholism, the American Psychiatric Association, and the American Academy of Family Practice. It is also considered a disease by the American Psychological Association, American Public Health Association, American Hospital Association, and the World Health Organization.

Even among those who have accepted alcoholism as a disease there has been a common belief that its primary cause is psychological. Dr. James Milam (6) (20) has made a major contribution to the recognition of alcoholism as a PRIMARY physical disease. Dr. Milam has strongly asserted that psychological and social factors play no stronger role in alcoholism than in any other chronic disease. He has challenged the notion that alcoholism is caused by psychological susceptibility and presented the view that the body of a person who becomes addicted to alcohol does not react to alcohol in the same way as a person who does not become addicted.

Research in recent years strongly supports this position. The research of Charles Leiber (31) (32), Marc Schuckit (34) (35), and others indicates that some people are born with a body more susceptible to addiction than other people.

While addiction is a primary physical disease, it is affected by and affects all areas of a person's life. For this reason we call addictive disease a biopsycho-social disease. "Bio" means biological or of the body. "Psycho" means psychological or of the mind. "Social" refers to relationships among people. (5)

Addictive disease is bio-psycho-social.

The study of brain chemicals that affect the transmission of messages by nerve cells is advancing the understanding of addiction. But many of the answers that are being discovered are also raising new questions. The whole process of chemical action in the brain is very complex, but it is very clear that brain chemistry in an addicted person differs from that of a nonaddicted person. (21)

Much is being learned also from liver metabolism studies which show that many people with a family history of alcoholism metabolize alcohol (break it down and eliminate it from the body) differently even before there is any indication of problem drinking. (34)

These studies strongly support a genetic and hereditary basis for addiction. People with a genetic predisposition for alcoholism are not predestined to develop the disease, but they are in high risk because of the way their bodies respond to alcohol. (25) (26) (27) (29)

A person must use alcohol or drugs to become addicted. The extent of genetic predisposition will influence how much alcohol and drug use over what period of time will be necessary to trigger addiction. Different people have different levels of genetic or inherited susceptibility to addiction. In some persons a small amount of alcohol or drug use over a short period of time will trigger the addiction. Other people must use alcohol and drugs heavily for a long period of time for addictive disease to develop. (28)

Jack began to use alcohol at age 19. The first time he used alcohol he drank more than he intended to, got drunk, and got into trouble because of his drinking. Jack never had a day of normal drinking. By age 26, only seven years after his first drink, Jack was in the hospital seriously ill from his alcoholism. Later in his AA talk, Jack would describe himself as an "instant alcoholic."

Bill, on the other hand, also began drinking at age 19. He seldom got drunk. His first noticeable problems with alcohol began at age 34. Alcohol use didn't cause serious problems until he was 46. Bill had 15 years of seemingly normal drinking before his alcoholism became apparent.

People begin to use alcohol or drugs for **psychosocial** reasons. They drink because it makes them feel good (a psychological reason), because other people do, because it helps them to belong, or because they are pressured to do so (social reasons).

People become addicted for **physical** reasons. They develop tolerance; it takes more of the drug to produce the same effect. The cells of the body adapt to high levels of the drug and begin to function normally when it is present. This leads to dependence. The body comes to need the drug; absence of the drug will result in physical withdrawal causing discomfort and illness.

The more people use chemicals to feel good, the less they learn to use more effective ways to experience and cope with feelings, situations, and people. They do not learn—or they forget to use-other methods of coping. Their dependence has become psycho-social as well as physical. All life areas are affected.

WITHDRAWAL

The pain that develops when an addicted person stops using alcohol or drugs is called withdrawal. Withdrawal is bio-psycho-social. Part of the pain of withdrawal is created by physical damage and the body's need for the addictive substance. Part of the pain is caused by a psychological reaction to losing the primary method of coping with life—the use of addictive drugs. Part of the pain is social, caused by the separation from an addiction-centered lifestyle.

Physical withdrawal develops in two phases. The first is called acute withdrawal and lasts for three to ten days. (20) At one time people believed that the pain of withdrawal passed within several days. Recent research, however, indicates that withdrawal is longterm and may last for months or even years into sobriety. (125) (108) (122) This long-term withdrawal, called post acute withdrawal (PAW) will be discussed in detail in a later chapter.

PROGRESSION

An alcoholic will develop a predictable series of alcohol-and drug-based symptoms. (15) (17) (19) (20) These symptoms progress through three stages. (17) In the early stage it is very difficult to distinguish addictive from nonaddictive use because there are few outward symptoms. The body, however, is changing and adapting to the regular ingestion of the drug. The major symptom of early stage addiction is an increasing tolerance. This means that people who are becoming addicted can usually use larger and larger quantities without becoming intoxicated and without suffering harmful consequences.

ADDICTIVE DISEASE PROGRESSION

1. Early Stage—growing tolerance and dependency
2. Middle Stage—progressive loss of control
3. Chronic Stage—deterioration of bio-psycho-social health

It is difficult for these people to recognize that they are addicted because they can "handle their liquor" (or marijuana or Valium). The earliest warning sign, then, actually thwarts early diagnosis because it conceals the problem. While most diseases create immediate impairments in functioning, this disease appears in the early stage as a benefit, enabling the affected person to enjoy the euphoria of drug use without paying any of the penalties.

All the while, physical and psychological dependence—though hidden—is growing so there is no longer just a desire to use but a need to use. As cells of the liver and nervous system change in order to tolerate larger quantities of the chemical, even larger amounts are needed to achieve the same effect. Increased quantities damage the liver and alter brain chemistry, and eventually tolerance begins to decrease.

Bill was amazed when he finally started into treatment. "I didn't believe how seriously ill I was," said Bill. "The problem snuck up on me an inch at a time. The changes were so slow I never realize how destructive my drinking had become."

The middle stage of addiction, then, is marked by a progressive loss of control as the person is no longer able to use the same quantities without becoming intoxicated or creating problems. Not using begins to create pain. The drug is used to relieve the pain created by not using. The addicted person is unable to function normally without the drug.

Family and friends begin to notice problems: job, health, marriage, legal problems. They are apt to believe, however, that the person is just behaving irresponsibly. They are not aware that the addicted person is not choosing the problem behavior. It is part of the disease. The person cannot, through willpower, choose to drink or use responsibly. The only alternative to continued problems and progression of the disease process is treatment and total abstinence.

The chronic stage of addiction is marked by deterioration—physical, psychological, behavioral, social, and spiritual. All body systems can be affected at this stage. The brain, the liver, the heart, and the digestive system are often damaged. Mood swings are common as the person uses the drug to feel better but is unable to maintain the good feelings. As life becomes more and more drug centered, there is less and less control over behavior. Activities that interfere with drinking or using are given up. Getting ready to use, using, and recovering from using become the life activities of addicted people. They do things while drinking they would not do sober. While sober, they structure their lives to protect their using. They break promises, forget commitments, lie—all to be able to use. Isolation is common. Friends and acquaintances separate themselves because behavior becomes embarrassing or offensive. Life is consumed by the need to use. Drug seeking behavior becomes a lifestyle.

THE BASIS OF DENIAL

1. ***Early Stage—few observable problems.***
2. ***Middle State— problems not associated with addictive use.***
3. ***Chronic Stage—too sick to think rationally.***

DELUSIONAL THINKING

Addiction is a chronic disease. It comes on gradually and allows addicted persons to adjust to the illness so that, for a while, they are able to continue functioning even though ill. Because they are not aware that they are compensating for and adapting to their illness, they are able to deny they are sick for a long time. Denial of the illness is increased by neurological impairments that distort reality, by blackouts that create blank spots in the memory, and by the effect of intoxication on perception and memory. Denial of the disease is part of the disease.

The addicted person is able to deny the existence of the addiction because in the early stage there are no physical or behavioral problems; in the middle stage problems are not associated with using; and in the chronic stage thinking is impaired and judgment distorted. Denial blocks motivation for recovery by masking the painful reality of a life caught in a cycle of pain, denial, and alcohol/drug use from which there seems to be no way out. (62) (63) (66)

THE ADDICTION CYCLE

What we have described is a cycle of addiction that leads the addicted person into a deadly trap. Let's take a closer look at this cycle and what happens to you if you become trapped in it.

ADDICTION CYCLE

1. ***Short-term gratification***
2. ***Long-term pain***
3. ***Addictive thinking***
4. ***Increased tolerance***
5. ***Loss of control***
6. ***Bio-psycho-social damage***

1. SHORT-TERM GRATIFICATION: First there is shortterm gratification. You feel good now. There is a strong short-term gain that causes you to assume the drug or behavior is good for you.

2. LONG-TERM PAIN AND DYSFUNCTION: The short-term gratification is eventually followed by long-term pain. This pain, part of which is from physical withdrawal, and part of which is from the inability to cope psycho-socially without drugs, is the direct consequence of using the addictive drugs.

3. ADDICTIVE THINKING: The long-term pain and dysfunction trigger addictive thinking. Addictive thinking begins with ***obsession*** and ***compulsion***. Obsession is a continuous thinking about the positive effects of using alcohol and drugs. Compulsion is an irrational urge or craving to use the drug to get the positive effect even though you know it will hurt you in the long run. This leads to ***denial*** and ***rationalization*** in order to allow continued use. Denial is the inability to recognize there is a problem. Rationalization is blaming other situations and people for problems rather than drug use.

4. INCREASED TOLERANCE: Without your being aware that it is happening, more and more of the drug is required to produce the same effect.

5. LOSS OF CONTROL: The obsession and compulsion become so strong that you cannot think about anything else. Your feelings and emotions become distorted by the compulsion. You become stressed and uncomfortable until finally the urge to use is so strong

that you cannot resist it. Once you use the addictive chemicals or the addictive behaviors again, the cycle starts all over.

6. BIO-PSYCHO-SOCIAL DAMAGE: Eventually there is damage to the health of your body (physical health), mind (psychological health), and relationships with other people (social health). As pain and stress get worse, the compulsion to use the addictive drugs or behaviors to get relief from the pain increases. A deadly trap develops. You need addictive use in order to feel good. When you use addictively you damage yourself physically, psychologically, and socially. This damage increases your pain which increases your need for addictive use.

RECOVERY

Total abstinence is necessary to recover from an addiction. Promises to cut down are promises that cannot be kept. Any use will keep the addiction active. Abstinence is a necessary first step for recovery.

Susan rebelled at the need for total abstinence. "I thought I could control my use," she said in telling her story. She struggled with control for five years before she accepted the need for total abstinence. "I worked harder at controlling my alcohol and drug use than I ever worked at anything in my entire life. And even with all of that work I would periodically fail and get in trouble. I finally had to ask myself why is control is important? The answer was simple. Because I'm chemically dependent and must protect my right to use at all costs."

Abstinence alone, however, is not recovery. In most instances a choice to stop using is not sufficient to bring about long-term sobriety and recovery unless the decision is accompanied by treatment of some type. Many well-intentioned chemically dependent people have made honest attempts to quit using but, without help outside of themselves, they have not been successful.

The first step in treatment is detoxification, removing the toxic substance from the body. Acute withdrawal symptoms that emerge when the chemical is removed can be very serious. Withdrawal is a medical problem and should be treated by a physician. A common method of detoxification is administering a substitute drug and gradually decreasing the dose until the withdrawal symptoms have subsided. It should be noted that the person is not fully detoxified until the substitute drug has also been removed and the person is drug free.

Detox alone is not adequate treatment for addictive disease.

Detoxification alone is not adequate treatment. In order to maintain abstinence, much more is required. Addiction affects all aspects of a person's life. Therefore, this disease requires wholistic treatment. Recovery requires long-term physical, psychological, behavioral, social, and spiritual change. Education is an important aspect of treatment. Because recovery from an addiction requires self-management, it is essential for addiction patients to learn as much as possible about their disease and how it is manages.

Individual and group counseling—in a hospital inpatient or outpatient program or a nonhospital residential setting—are vital components of treatment. The intent of counseling is to facilitate the development of skills that will support ongoing sobriety and long-term recovery. Searching for the cause of an addiction (such as emotional or family problems) is usually nonproductive. Treatment that recognizes the addiction as a primary condition rather than a symptom of something else, has been found to be most effective.

Alcoholics Anonymous is the single most effective treatment for alcoholism. More people have recovered from alcoholism using the program of AA than have recovered using any other form of treatment. It is for this reason that AA needs to be a vital part of any recovering alcoholic's sobriety plan. There are similar self-help groups for other addictions.

In early recovery, however, most people require more extensive or more specialized help than a selfhelp group alone can provide. When people are physically ill, they need medical care. Some people need to be in a protective environment in order to maintain abstinence long enough for recovery to begin.

The most successful treatment combines the Twelve Steps principles of AA with professional counseling and therapy.

There are also many times in the course of recovery that the recovering person will confront specialized problems. These may include financial difficulties, marital problems, emotional or psychological disorders, or behavioral problems that are the direct result of addiction. While these will usually improve with a self-help program alone, it has been demonstrated that professional counseling and therapy can provide assistance in resolving these issues more rapidly and effectively. The most successful form of treatment combines a self-help group with professional treatment.

Management of long-term withdrawal symptoms is essential to maintaining sobriety. Management includes understanding and accepting these symptoms that interfere with the ability to remember, think clearly, and manage feelings and emotions. It also includes overcoming the shame, guilt, and fear of being crazy that are often associated with these symptoms. It includes reducing and managing stress, memory retraining, and balanced living.

Sobriety is essential for good health and good health is essential for sobriety. The first rule of good physical health for a recovering person includes abstaining from all mood-altering drugs. This includes over-the-counter and prescription drugs, unless they are absolutely necessary to manage another serious health problem. Then they should be very carefully monitored under the care of a physician and an addictions counselor.

Good nutrition is vital for recovery. Malnutrition and alcohol or drugs have damaged the body, and it must be rebuilt through a balanced diet. Because recovering people are stress sensitive, stressproducing substances such as concentrated sweets, caffeine and nicotine, should be avoided. Exercise is important to help rebuild and maintain the body. Aerobic exercise is especially beneficial in reducing and managing stress. Time for relaxation should be structured into the life of every recovering person. Relaxation exercises rebalance the body and reduce the production of stress hormones. Fun and play are also relaxing and contribute to health and well being.

Recovery requires resolution of family, work, and social problems that were created by an active addiction. It also involves the development of new and more meaningful social networks. Family members must be part of the recovery program. They, as well as the user, have been made dysfunctional by drug use. Roles, rules, and rituals of the family must be redefined and restructured. Communication skills must be learned or relearned in sobriety. The whole family needs to recover together.

It is difficult to recover from an addiction without what is referred to in AA as a "spiritual program." The principles of AA teach that alcoholics are powerless over their condition and cannot manage their lives until they accept the help of a power greater than themselves. A life that includes wholesome living, uplifting relationships, commitment to values outside of oneself, and spiritual growth supports long-term health and sobriety. Reorienting life around values that are non-drug centered is an essential part of recovery. A lifestyle conducive to using is not conducive to sobriety.

Chapter III

POST ACUTE WITHDRAWAL

When most people think about alcoholism they think only of the alcohol-based symptoms and forget about the sobriety-based symptoms. Yet it is the sobrietybased symptoms, especially post acute withdrawal, that make sobriety so difficult. The presence of brain dysfunction has been documented in 75–95% of recovering alcoholics tested. (150) Recent research indicates that the symptoms of long-term withdrawal associated with alcohol- and drug-related damage to the brain may contribute to many cases of relapse. (141) (105)

Post acute withdrawal means symptoms that occur after acute withdrawal. ***Post*** means ***after***. And ***syndrome*** means ***a group of symptoms.***

Syndrome: A group of symptoms
Post: After
Post Acute Withdrawal: Symptoms that occur after acute withdrawal.

Post acute withdrawal is a group of symptoms of addictive disease that occur as a result of abstinence from addictive chemicals. In the alcoholic these symptoms appear seven to fourteen days into abstinence, after stabilization from the acute withdrawal.

Post acute withdrawal is a bio-psycho-social syndrome. It results from the combination of damage to the nervous system caused by alcohol or drugs and the psycho-social stress of coping with life without drugs or alcohol.

Recovery causes a great deal of stress. Many chemically dependent people never learn to manage stress without alcohol and drug use. The stress aggravates the brain dysfunction and makes the symptoms worse. (39) (40) The severity of PAW depends upon two things: the severity of the brain dysfunction caused by the addiction and the amount of psychosocial stress experienced in recovery.

The symptoms of PAW usually grow to a peak intensity over three to six months after abstinence begins. The damage is usually reversible, meaning the major symptoms go away in time if proper treatment is received. So there is no need to fear. With proper treatment and effective sober living, it is possible to learn to live normally in spite of the impairments. But the adjustment does not occur rapidly. Recovery from the nervous system damage usually requires from six to 24 months with the assistance of a healthy recovery program.

SYMPTOMS OF POST ACUTE WITHDRAWAL

How do you know if you have PAW? The most identifiable characteristic is the inability to solve usually simple problems. There are six major types of PAW symptoms that contribute to this. They are the inability to think clearly, emotional overreactions, memory problems, sleep disturbances, physical coordination problems, and problems in managing stress because of any or all of these symptoms leads to diminished self-esteem. A person feels incompetent, embarrassed, and "not OK" about self. Diminished selfesteem and fear of failure interfere with productive and challenging living. Let's take a look at some of the PAW symptoms that contribute to the inability to solve usually simple problems.

TYPES OF PAW SYMPTOMS

1. ***Inability to think clearly***
2. ***Memory problems***
3. ***Emotional overreactions or numbness***
4. ***Sleep disturbances***
5. ***Physical coordination problems***
6. ***Stress sensitivity***

Inability to Think Clearly

There are several thought disorders experienced by a recovering person when PAW is activated. Intelligence is not affected. It is as if the brain is malfunctioning ***sometimes.*** Sometimes it works all right. Sometimes it does not.

One of the most common symptoms is the inability to concentrate for more than a few minutes. Impairment of abstract reasoning is another common symptom of post acute withdrawal. An abstraction is a nonconcrete idea or concept, something that you cannot hold in your hand, take a picture of, or put in a box. Concentration is more of a problem when abstract concepts are involved.

Another common symptom is rigid and repetitive thinking. The same thoughts may go around and around in your head and you are unable to break through this circular thinking in order to put thoughts together in an orderly way.

Memory Problems

Short-term memory problems are very common in the recovering person. You may hear something and understand it, but within 20 minutes you forget it. Someone will give an instruction and you know exactly what to do. But you may walk away, and that memory becomes clouded or may disappear completely.

Sometimes during stressful periods it may also be difficult to remember significant events from the past. These memories are not gone; the person may be able to remember them easily at other times. The person realizes that he or she knows but just cannot recall it while experiencing the stress.

For an alcoholic named Jan this created a problem in AA. "I have trouble presenting my story at AA," she said. "I have trouble remembering events that happened before my drinking days, let alone things that happened while I was drinking. So to put my life in story form is hard for me. I don't remember all of my story. I do remember that some things occurred, but I get confused about when they happened. Many times I can remember things when I am alone with no pressure that I can't remember under the stress I feel when I talk at meetings."

Because of memory problems in recovery, it may be difficult to learn new skills and information. You learn skills by acquiring knowledge and building upon what you have already learned. Memory problems make it difficult to build upon what you have already learned.

Emotional Overreaction or Numbness

Persons with emotional problems in sobriety tend to overreact. When things happen that require two units of emotional reaction, they react with ten. It is like holding the "times" key down on a calculator. You may find yourself becoming angry over what may later seem a trivial matter. You may feel more anxious or excited than you have reason to be. When this overreaction puts more stress on the nervous system than it can handle, there is an emotional shutdown. If this happens to you, you become emotionally numb, unable to feel anything. And even when you know you should feel something, you do not. You may swing from one mood to another without knowing why.

Sleep Problems

Most recovering people experience sleep problems. Some of them are temporary; some are lifelong. The most common in early recovery is unusual or disturbing dreams. These dreams may interfere with your ability to get the sleep you need. But they become less frequent and less severe as the length of abstinence increases.

Mike was a periodic drinker. Periods of sobriety usually lasted for several months. During the time he was not drinking, he had dreams that severely disrupted his sleep. His wife said, "I never realized the nightmares Mike was having had anything to do with drinking or not drinking. He would frequently jump up out of bed, screaming in terror. When I was able to awaken him and calm him, he couldn't remember what he dreamed, but he remembered being afraid. After a year of sobriety, he seldom had the dreams. Only then did I realize that they were related to his drinking."

Even if you do not experience unusual dreams, you may have difficulty falling asleep or staying asleep. You may experience changes in your sleep patterns; sleeping for long periods at a time or sleeping at different times of the day. Some of these patterns may never return to "normal," but most people are able to adjust to them without severe difficulty.

Physical Coordination Problems

A very serious PAW problem—though perhaps not as common as the others—is difficulty with physical coordination. Common symptoms are dizziness, trouble with balance, problems with coordination between hand and eye, and slow reflexes. These result in clumsiness and accident proneness. This is how the term "dry drunk" came into being. When alcoholics appeared drunk because of stumbling and clumsiness, but had not been drinking, they were said to be "dry drunk." They had the appearance of being intoxicated without drinking.

Stress Sensitivity

Difficulty in managing stress is the most confusing and aggravating part of post acute withdrawal. Recovering people are often unable to distinguish between low-stress situations and highstress situations. They may not recognize low levels of stress, and then overreact when they become aware of the stress they are experiencing. They may feel stressful in situations that ordinarily would not bother them, and in addition, when they react they overreact. They may do things that are completely inappropriate for the situation. So much so that later on they may wonder why they reacted so strongly.

To complicate things further, all of the other symptoms of post acute withdrawal become worse during times of high stress. There is a direct relationship between elevated stress and the severity of PAW. Each intensifies the other. The intensity of PAW creates stress, and stress aggravates PAW and makes it more severe. At times of low stress, the symptoms get better and **may even go away**. When you are well rested and relaxed, eating properly, and getting along well with people, you will probably appear to be fine. Your thoughts will be clear, your emotions appropriate, and your memory all right. At times of high stress, however, your brain may suddenly shut down. You may begin experiencing thinking problems, inappropriate emotions, and memory problems.

If your thoughts become confused and chaotic or you are unable to concentrate, if you have trouble remembering or solving problems, you may feel you are going crazy. You are not. These symptoms are a normal part of your recovery and are reversible with abstinence and a recovery program. If you do not understand this you may develop shame and guilt which leads to diminished self-esteem and isolation which creates stress and increased PAW. It is a painful cycle that is unnecessary if you understand what is happening. As your body and your mind begin to heal and as you learn ways to reduce the risk of post acute withdrawal symptoms, productive and meaningful living is possible in spite of the very real possibility of recurring symptoms.

Recovery from the damage caused by the addiction requires abstinence. The damage itself interferes with the ability to abstain. This is the paradox of recovery. Alcohol can temporarily reverse the symptoms of the damage. If alcoholics drink, they will think clearly for a little while, be able to have normal feelings and emotions for a little while, feel healthy for a little while. Unfortunately, the disease will eventually trigger a loss of control that will again destroy these functions.

For this reason it is necessary to do everything possible to reduce the symptoms of PAW. It is necessary to understand PAW and to recognize that you are not incompetent and you are not going crazy. Because post acute withdrawal symptoms are stress sensitive, you need to learn about PAW and methods of control when stress levels are low in order to be able to prevent the symptoms or to manage them when they occur.

Here are some stories about some people who experienced post acute withdrawal and how it affected their lives without their being aware of what was happening to them.

Ray is a young, single, recovering alcoholic. He stopped drinking when he was 22 and was very excited about the possibilities that lay ahead of him in his sobriety. After his initial treatment he began restructuring his life around recovery. He was eager to make up for the time he had wasted during his years of drinking. He got a full-time job, enrolled in college, and committed himself to doing some volunteer work.

After a while he began to notice that he was having trouble with his schoolwork. He found himself confused about things that had at one time been easy for him to follow and figure out. He was having trouble taking care of his financial responsibilities, and when people that cared about him tried to help him figure things out, he felt panicky and overwhelmed. Thoughts rushed through his head, and he was unable to put them in order. He says, "When someone in the financial aid office at the college started talking to me about grant money, loan money, interest, and forms that needed to be filled out, I was so confused and overwhelmed that I couldn't hear what she was saying. Everything was going around in my head at once and I had to get away. I got up and left without filling out the financial aid form."

In desperation, and out of fear that he would drink, Ray "ran." Instead of evaluating what things in his life he needed to change and what he needed to hold onto, he gave up everything. He quit his job, dropped out of school, and stopped doing volunteer work. He gave up his apartment and moved in with a relative until he could "get himself together." These actions created additional problems with which he found it increasingly difficult to cope. Until he went to a counselor and learned some ways to manage his symptoms, Ray thought he was having a nervous breakdown, when in fact what he was experiencing was PAW.

Thelma got a new job shortly after her initial recovery. She was confident in her ability to learn the job and function in her new responsibilities. She did not have any trouble understanding what she was supposed to do when it was explained to her. But a short time later when she attempted to do certain tasks by herself, she could not remember how to do them. She was embarrassed to ask for more help because she thought she should be able to do these simple tasks without help.

She frequently made mistakes when she tried to figure out by herself what needed to be done.

She began to feel very anxious, and as her stress increased, her memory problems increased. In addition, she began having trouble concentrating when someone explained things to her. She got confused and her anxiety increased. "I couldn't figure out what was happening to me," she complained. "I knew I had the ability to do the job. But the harder I tried, the worse it got. I was confused and upset and I didn't know where to go for help."

After a number of serious problems arose, Thelma lost her job. She was bewildered as to how this could have happened and began to believe that she was much less competent than she was.

PATTERNS OF POST ACUTE WITHDRAWAL

Post acute withdrawal symptoms are not the same in everyone. They vary in how severe they are, how often they occur, and how long they last. Some people experience certain symptoms; some people have other symptoms; some people have none at all. (126) (141)

Over a period of time PAW may get better, it may get worse, it may stay the same, or it may come and go. If it gets better with time we call it ***regenerative***. If it gets worse we call it ***degenerative***. If it stays the same we call it **stable**. And if it comes and goes we call it ***intermittent***.

Regenerative PAW gradually improves over time. The longer a person is sober the less severe the symptoms become. It is easier for people with regenerative PAW to recover because the brain rapidly returns to normal.

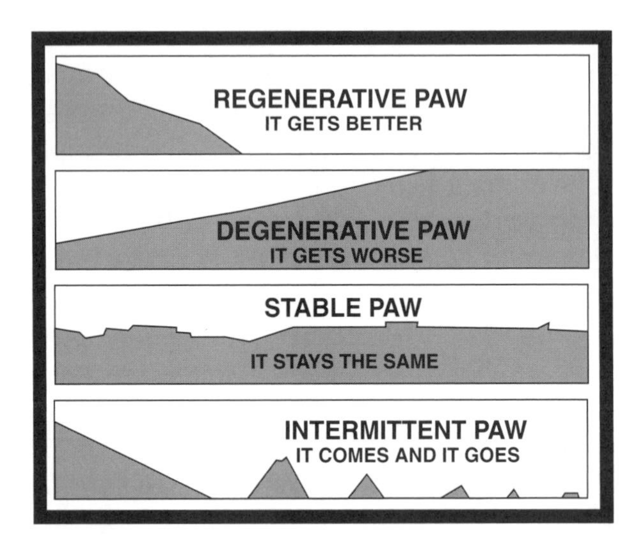

Degenerative PAW is the opposite. The symptoms get worse the longer a person is sober. This may happen even when a person is going to AA and/or following some type of recovery program. People with degenerative PAW tend to become relapse prone. Sobriety becomes so painful that they feel they must self-medicate the pain with alcohol or drugs, collapse physically or emotionally, or commit suicide to end the pain.

A person with stable PAW experiences the same level of symptoms for a long period of time into recovery. There may be days when the symptoms are a little better or a little worse, but essentially the symptoms remain unchanged. Most recovering people find this very frustrating because they believe that they should be feeling better the longer they are sober. With sufficient sober time many people learn to manage these symptoms.

With intermittent PAW the symptoms come and go. Initially people with intermittent symptoms will appear to experience a regenerative pattern. In other words, their symptoms rapidly get better. But then they begin to experience periodic PAW episodes that can be quite severe. For some people the episodes get shorter, less severe, and farther apart until they stop altogether. In others they occur periodically throughout life.

These patterns describe people who have not had treatment for PAW and who do not know how to manage or prevent the symptoms. Traditional treatment does not address these symptoms because until recently they were unrecognized. If you know what to do and you are willing to do it, degenerative PAW can be changed into stable, stable into regenerative, and regenerative into intermittent PAW.

The most common pattern of PAW is regenerative that over time becomes intermittent. It gradually gets better until the symptoms disappear and then it comes and goes. The first step is to bring PAW symptoms into remission. This means bringing them under control so that you are not experiencing them at the present time. Then the goal is to reduce how often they occur, how long the episode lasts, and how bad the symptoms are.

You must remember that even when you are not experiencing them there is always the tendency for them to recur. It is necessary to build a resistance against them—an insurance policy that lowers your risk.

MANAGING PAW SYMPTOMS

The less you do to strengthen yourself against an episode of post acute withdrawal, the weaker your resistance becomes. It is like a tetanus shot. The longer it has been since you have had one, the more risk there is that you will become seriously ill if you cut yourself on a piece of rusty metal. Conditions

that put you in high risk of experiencing post acute withdrawal symptoms are usually lack of care of yourself and lack of attention to your recovery program. If you are going to recover without relapse you need to be aware of stressful situations in your life that can increase your risk of experiencing PAW.

Since you cannot remove yourself from all stressful situations you need to prepare yourself to handle them when they occur. It is not the situation that makes you go to pieces; it is your reaction to the situation.

Because stress triggers and intensifies the symptoms of post acute withdrawal, PAW can be controlled by learning to manage stress. You can learn to identify sources of stress and develop skills in decision making and problem solving to help reduce stress. Proper diet, exercise, regular habits, and positive attitudes all play important parts in controlling PAW. Relaxation can be used as a tool to retrain the brain to function properly and to reduce stress.

Stabilization

If you are experiencing post acute withdrawal symptoms, it is important to bring them under control as soon as possible. Here are some suggestions that may help you be aware of what is going on and help you to interrupt the symptoms before they get out of control.

Verbalization: Start talking to people who are not going to accuse, criticize, or minimize. You need to talk about what you are experiencing. It will help you look at your situation more realistically. It will help you bring internal symptoms to your conscious awareness. And it will give you support when you need others to rely upon.

Ventilation: Express as much as you can about what you are thinking and feeling even if it seems irrational and unfounded.

Reality Testing: Ask someone if you are making sense. Not just what you are saying but your behavior. Your perception of what is going on may be very different from reality.

Problem Solving and Goal Setting: What are you going to do right now about what is going on? You can choose to take action that can change things.

Backtracking: Think back over what has been happening. Can you identify how the episode started? What could have turned it off sooner? Think of other times that you were experiencing symptoms of PAW. What turned it on? What turned it off? Were there other options that might have worked better or sooner?

Education and Retraining

Learning about addictive disease, recovery, and post acute withdrawal symptoms helps to relieve the anxiety, guilt, and confusion that tend to create the stress that intensify PAW symptoms. As a recovering person, you need information in order to realize that the symptoms are normal during recovery.

You also need to learn management skills so that you will know what to do to interrupt and control the stress and the symptoms when they occur. Through retraining you can improve your ability to remember, to concentrate, and to think clearly. Retraining involves practicing certain skills in a safe environment as you build confidence. It includes learning to take things step by step and to handle one thing at a time so you do not feel overwhelmed. It includes writing down what you want to remember and asking questions when you need to have something clarified.

Learning about the symptoms of post acute withdrawal, knowing what to expect, and not overreacting to the symptoms increase the ability to function appropriately and effectively.

Self-Protective Behavior

When all is said and done, you are responsible for protecting yourself from anything that threatens your sobriety or anything that triggers post acute withdrawal symptoms. Reducing the stress resulting from and contributing to the symptoms of post acute withdrawal should be of prime consideration for you. You must learn behavior that will protect you from the stress that might put your sobriety in jeopardy. This ***self-protective*** behavior is behavior that will enable you to be firm in accepting your own needs and not allowing other people or situations to push you into reactions that are not in the best interest of your sobriety.

In order to protect yourself from unnecessary stress, you must first identify your own stress triggers, those situations that might bring about an overreaction from you. Then learn to change those situations, avoid them, change your reactions, or learn to interrupt them before they get out of control.

Nutrition

The way you eat has a lot to do with the level of stress you experience and your ability to manage the symptoms of post acute withdrawal. Poor health itself contributes to stress, and malnutrition contributes to poor health. You may be malnourished because of poor eating habits or because your body, damaged by alcohol or drugs, was unable to use the nutrients that you consumed. (188)

Abstinence from alcohol and drugs will bring about some improvement but abstinence alone is not sufficient to rebuild damaged body tissue and maintain good health. New eating habits must be established and practiced regularly and permanently. (187) Your daily diet should contain a balance of vegetables, fruit, carbohydrates, proteins, fats, and milk products. Ask a nutritionist to help you figure out how many calories you need each day and what quantities of each type of food.

DIET FOR A RECOVERING PERSON
—Three Well-Balanced Meals Daily—
—Three Nutritious Snacks Daily—
—Avoid Sugar and Caffeine—

Hunger produces stress. Try to plan your eating schedule so that you do not skip meals and so that you can have periodic nutritious snacks. Do not eat candy, donuts, soft drinks, potato chips, or other high calorie, low nutrient foods. You should specifically avoid foods that produce stress such as concentrated sweets and caffeine. Both of these produce the same kind of chemical reaction in your body as being frightened or overly excited. Concentrated sweets such as candy, jelly, syrup, and sugar-sweetened soft drinks will give you a quick "pick-up," but you will experience a let-down about an hour later accompanied by nervousness and irritability.

Remember that your reason for eating a snack is to combat fatigue and nervousness. Have a nutritious snack before you feel hungry to prevent a craving for sweets.

Jayne, a recovering alcoholic, was in the habit of eating a large quantity of ice cream every night. She often talked about the craving for it she felt, and believed that by eating it she was reducing a craving for alcohol. The next morning she always felt sluggish and irritable. Throughout the day her stress increased until it was relieved by the ice cream. When her counselor suggested that she remove the ice cream from her diet she felt she could not get along without it. When she and her counselor examined her diet they found that she ate no breakfast and was not getting adequate nutrition throughout the day. She agreed to try eating a balanced diet and to eliminate the ice cream on a trial basis. She discovered that when she ate a balanced diet and ate regular meals and several nutritious snacks throughout the day her craving for ice cream disappeared and she could easily eliminate it from her life.

Caffeine also causes nervousness and restlessness. It may also interfere with concentration and your ability to sleep. Loss of sleep or irregular sleep causes irritability, depression, and anxiety. (96) (101)

Exercise

Exercise helps rebuild the body and keep it functioning properly while also reducing stress. Exercise produces chemicals in your brain that make you feel good. These chemicals are nature's own tranquilizers to relieve pain, anxiety, and tension. (45) (46)

Different types of exercise are helpful for different reasons. Stretching and aerobic exercise will probably be most helpful for your recovery. Stretching exercises help to keep your body limber and to relieve muscle tension. Aerobics are rhythmical and vigorous exercises for the large muscles. Aerobics are intended to raise your heart rate to 75% of its maximum rate and maintain that rate for at least 20–30 minutes.

We recommend regular use of aerobic exercise. Jogging, swimming, jumping rope, and bicycling are common aerobic exercises, or you might want to join an aerobics class. Dancing can also be aerobic, but remember that it must be done vigorously.

Many recovering people will testify to the value of exercise in reducing the intensity of PAW symptoms. After they exercise they feel much better, find it easier to concentrate and remember, and are able to be more productive.

Choose a form of exercise that is fun for you so that you will stick with it. Most doctors and health books will tell you to exercise three or four times a week, but we recommend that recovering people make time for it every day because of its value in reducing stress. Any day that you do not exercise is a day that you are cheating yourself of a way to feel more relaxed, be more productive, and have more energy.

Relaxation

There are things you can do to readily reduce or escape the stress you feel when you are unable to change a situation or to better cope with the stress of everyday living. Laughing, playing, listening to music, story telling, fantasizing, reading, and massage are some methods of natural stress reduction. (174)

Playing is a necessary form of relaxation that is often neglected. It is difficult to define play because it is not so much what you do as how you do it. We all need time for having fun, laughing, being childlike and free. There are other "diversions" you can use as natural stress reducers. Try body massage, a bubble bath, a walk by yourself or with a friend.

Deep relaxation is a way of relaxing the body and mind to reduce stress and produce a sense of well-being. Deep relaxation rebalances the body and reduces the production of stress hormones. What happens when you relax is the opposite of the "fight or flight" reaction. When you relax, your muscles become heavy, your body temperature rises, and your breathing and heart rate slow down. A muscle cannot relax and tense at the same time. It is impossible to maintain tension while physically relaxing. You can learn techniques to allow your body to relax. The distress resulting from thought process impairments, emotional process impairments, memory impairments, and stress sensitivity can be reduced or relieved through proper use of relaxation.

There are a variety of relaxation exercises that you can use. You can get a book that will offer you a selection of exercises or you can purchase tape recorded exercises. You can close your eyes in a comfortable position and repeat a pleasant word over and over to yourself. Or you can imagine yourself in a soothing environment such as by a quiet lake or in a green meadow. Pick a method that is relaxing to you and use it often. You will find it a helpful aid for reducing stress and creating peace of mind and serenity. (40)

Spirituality

Spirituality is an active relationship with a power greater than yourself that gives your life meaning and purpose. When you work a spiritual program, you consciously, actively attempt to become a part of something bigger, greater, and more powerful than yourself.

Belief in a Higher Power takes you out of the center of your universe and offers peace of mind and serenity by an awareness that there is a power that is not restricted by your weaknesses and limitations. Through spiritual development you can develop new confidence in your own abilities and develop a new sense of hope. It is through a spiritual program that you can reach with hope and a positive attitude toward the future.

In working on your spirituality it is important for you to use the principles of the AA program. AA provides guidelines for "increasing your conscious contact with God." You do not have to have any one image of God to increase your conscious contact. You do have to be open to the possibility of a Higher Power and be willing to experiment with communicating with that Power. It is important to structure your life in such a way as to spend time alone each day to interact with your Higher Power. It is important to examine your values and look within yourself to determine whether your life is in harmony with those values.

Spiritual discipline is a consciously chosen course of action. Discipline is uncomfortable for many recovering addicts. They have lived lives of immediate gratification, and discipline is the reverse of that. The purpose of spiritual discipline is freedom from the slavery of self-indulgence. Spiritual discipline includes prayer and meditation, spiritual fellowship, and regular inventory of your spiritual growth.

Balanced Living

Balanced living means that there is bio-psychosocial harmony in your life. It means that you are healthy physically and psychologically and that you have healthy relationships. It means that you are spiritually whole. It means that you are no longer focused on one aspect of your life. It means you are living responsibly, giving yourself time for your job, your family, your friends as well as time for your own growth and recovery. It means allowing a Higher Power to work in your life. It means wholesome living.

It means having a balance between work and play,

between fulfilling your responsibilities to other people and your need for self-fulfillment. It means functioning as nearly as possible at your optimum stress level, maintaining enough stress to keep you functioning in a healthy way and not overloading yourself with stress so that it becomes counterproductive. With balanced living, immediate gratification as a lifestyle is given up in order to attain fulfilling and meaningful living.

Balanced living requires proper health care so that the body is functioning well. Nutrition, rest, and exercise all receive the proper focus in your life to provide energy, manage stress, allow freedom from illness and pain, combat fatigue, and rebuild a damaged body.

Freedom from physical distress allows psychological growth. When you feel good it is easier to think about your attitudes and values and to work on eliminating denial, guilt, and anger. Balanced living requires doing things to develop selfconfidence and self-esteem and learning to feel good about yourself.

Balanced living needs a strong social network that nurtures you and encourages a healthy, recoveryoriented lifestyle. A healthy network provides a sense of belonging. It includes relationships in which you feel you are a valuable part. It includes immediate family members, friends, relatives, co-workers, counselors, employers, self-help group members, and sponsors.

Even after a couple of years of sobriety, Walter had times when he found it more difficult than usual to re-

member things, when he was more irritable and anxious, when he overreacted around his family and friends, when he felt confused and overwhelmed. His wife began to notice that he experienced these symptoms more on Saturday. What was different about Saturday? He usually slept later and had a couple of cups of coffee as soon as he was awake. Because he felt irritable as soon as he got up, he began going over to visit his AA sponsor as early as possible. Together they drank coffee, ate donuts, smoked their pipes, and talked. Walter stayed until early afternoon, and by the time he got home and had lunch it was usually 1:30 or 2:00 in the afternoon. If one of his kids left a bike in the driveway or his wife was on the phone too long, he found himself overreacting and leaving the house. The rest of the day was totally unproductive because of what became known in his family as his "Saturday Syndrome."

Walter decided to try some alternate activities to see if there was a change in his reactions. He started drinking orange juice as soon as he woke up instead of coffee. That helped, so he decided to try eating breakfast. That helped even more. He and his sponsor started drinking decaffeinated coffee and he skipped the donuts. He came home early enough to have lunch and to exercise for awhile. He then felt like doing something with his family in the afternoon. They were all amazed at the disappearance of the "Saturday Syndrome."

Chapter IV

RECOVERY AND PARTIAL RECOVERY

Although addictive disease can be controlled, it can never be cured. There is always the possibility of relapse. Unless measures are taken on a long-term basis to control the disease, relapse is likely.

The first task of recovery is for alcoholics to recognize that they have a debilitating, lifethreatening disease associated with the use of alcohol or other mood-altering drugs. They must recognize that they have a disease that is impairing their ability to stay sober and to live productively.

Once this recognition is achieved, the second task of recovery is abstinence. Total abstinence is necessary. This means no alcohol in any form; no sleeping pills, sedatives, or mood-altering drugs.

The third task is to recognize the need for a daily program of recovery in order to give support and assistance in staying sober one day at a time.

Recovery from addictive disease is a process that requires a long period of time. A recent research study indicates that it takes eight to ten years for the average recovering alcoholic to fully return to normal. The most serious problems caused by the addiction require two to three years to resolve. The more longstanding lifestyle problems require eight to ten years for full resolution. (117)

The recovery process is developmental. This means that recovery is a process of growth and development that progresses from basic to complex recovery tasks. This progression is from ***abstinence*** (learning how to stop using alcohol and drugs) to ***sobriety*** (learning how to cope with life without alcohol and drugs), to ***comfortable living*** (learning how to live comfortably while abstinent), to ***productive living*** (learning how to build a meaningful sober lifestyle).*

It is helpful to think about the recovery process as having six developmental periods. (174) Each developmental period has a primary goal. Each period of recovery and its primary goal is listed below:

Developmental Period	***Goal***
1. Pretreatment	**Recognition of Addiction**
2. Stabilization	**Withdrawal and Crisis Management**
3. Early Recovery	**Acceptance and Non-chemical Coping**
4. Middle Recovery	**Balanced Living**
5. Late Recovery	**Personality Change**
6. Maintenance	**Growth and Development**

---

*See all references under *Developmental Model of Recovery* in the Bibliography.

The Developmental Model of Recovery (DMR) suggests that successful recovery is dependent upon completing specific recovery tasks in a specific order. Failure to complete certain recovery tasks will leave you unprepared to cope with more complex recovery tasks. You must remember that recovery is a very individual process. No two people recover in exactly the same way. What we are describing should be viewed as general guidelines not as an absolute picture of recovery for you. With this in mind the developmental periods of the DMR will be reviewed.

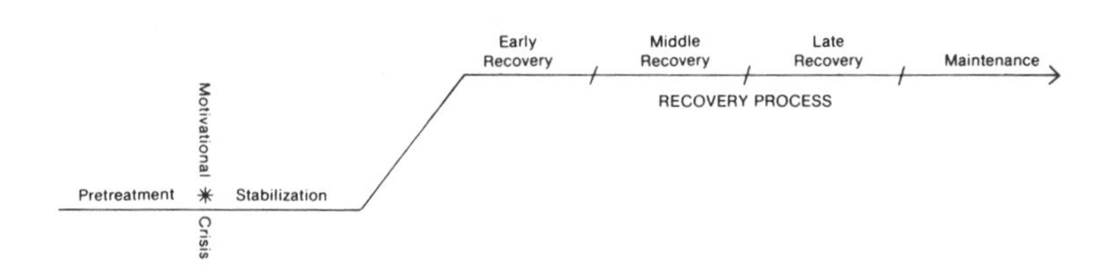

Diagram 1: The Recovery Process.
Partial recovery begins as a person progresses through the normal developmental stages of recovery.

THE PRETREATMENT PERIOD

The primary goal of pretreatment is recognizing the presence of addictive disease. You must recognize that you have lost the ability to control alcohol and drug use and are no longer a normal user but an addicted user. (170)

During this period you learn by the consequences of your behavior that you cannot safely use alcohol or drugs. This learning occurs as you develop problems associated with addictive use. As problems become more severe you attempt to control your using. (174) You may switch from bourbon to wine and then from wine to beer. You may use other drugs such as marijuana or amphetamines to offset the intoxicating effect of alcohol. When these things fail you attempt periods of sobriety to prove to yourself that you can control. (177) Finally defeat is admitted and you recognize you are an addicted user and cannot control your use.

It is important to understand that pretreatment describes the process going on within the chemically dependent person. It can, and does, take place sometimes after a person has been exposed to external treatment. It is possible, for example, for a person to be forced into treatment as a result of driving while intoxicated before ever having recognized that drinking is a problem. The recognition of addiction that comes as a result of treatment is, for the person, part of the pretreatment experience.

PRETREATMENT: Learning by the consequences *that you cannot safely use addictive chemicals.*

THE STABILIZATION PERIOD

During the stabilization period the major goal is to regain control of thought processes, emotional processes, judgment, and behavior. You are not stable until you are able to think clearly, identify and recognize feelings, remember things, exercise judgment, and control behavior. Stabilization involves recovery from acute withdrawal and severe symptoms of post acute withdrawal (PAW). It involves stabilization of the motivational crisis that prompted entry into treatment. It also involves the management of other acute physical and psycho-social problems that can jeopardize early recovery. During stabilization the pattern of addictive use is interrupted; symptoms of acute withdrawal, the immediate severe symptoms of post acute withdrawal, and physical health problems associated with the addiction are brought under control; and the major life crisis that caused the motivational crisis is stabilized.

STABILIZATION: Regaining control of thought processes, emotional processes, memory, judgment, and behavior.

THE EARLY RECOVERY PERIOD

During the early recovery period the major goal is accepting the disease of addiction and learning how to function without drugs and alcohol. A return to health is promoted by recuperation from the serious physical and psycho-social damage caused by addictive disease. This period of recuperation relies very heavily upon a structured recovery program that protects you from excessive stresses of day-to-day living. During this time you come to value sober living.

The structured recovery program allows for a period of physical healing to occur. A program of proper nutrition and stress management are established to provide relief from the symptoms of Post Acute Withdrawal (PAW). Physical treatment is provided for any co-existing physical illness or health problems.

The structured recovery program creates an environment that allows you and your family to become educated about addictive disease and recovery. It allows self-assessment about the nature and severity of your addiction and co-addiction patterns. It helps you to recognize and accept the addiction and resulting life problems and to begin to resolve those problems.

This structured recovery program is temporary. Its duration will vary, depending upon the severity of the addictive disease and the level of health and psycho-social problems. The goal is to teach you how to live as normally as possible with the use of a recovery program. If you break a leg, a temporary cast is required to restrict movement and promote healing. When you have damaged your personality and lifestyle as a result of addictive disease, a structured recovery program is necessary to restrict unnecessary stress and distraction from recovery while healing occurs. Once this initial healing has occurred, total abstinence, sobriety and productive living can be maintained with a far less restrictive recovery program than that required during stabilization and early recovery.

EARLY RECOVERY: Accepting the disease of addiction and learning to function without drugs and alcohol.

THE MIDDLE RECOVERY PERIOD

During the middle recovery period the primary goal is lifestyle change. You have established an addiction-centered lifestyle, a lifestyle that requires the use of addictive chemicals in order to manage the stress that has resulted from the addiction. In early recovery your addictive lifestyle was replaced by a structured recovery program that was developed by treatment people helping you to begin recovery. In middle recovery the challenge is to gradually develop a normal balanced lifestyle that is sobriety centered.

You are well and stable and you have worked through the issue of acceptance of your addiction. You are ready to being reducing your hours in therapy and to establish a pattern of normal living. Instead of focusing on not using, you focus on normal life issues, your job, and your family.

As an addicted person it is typical for you to establish an addiction-centered lifestyle, even though you are now abstinent. This is accomplished by using other addictions in the place of the original addiction. The goal is to establish a balanced lifestyle that is addiction free and based upon sobriety-centered values and activities.

Balanced living involves a recovery program that is active but less intense than in early recovery. It includes work activities, family activities, social activities with family and friends, time for selfdevelopment and recreation, and time for proper exercise and diet. Managing stress and resisting the urge for substitute addictions are important issues in middle recovery.

MIDDLE RECOVERY: Developing a normal, balanced lifestyle.

THE LATE RECOVERY PERIOD

The primary goal of the late recovery period is personality change for the development of healthy self-esteem, the capacity for healthy intimacy, and the ability to live happily and productively. It is time to evaluate personal values; beliefs about self, others, and the world; self-defeating patterns of living; intimacy and relationship skills. If these are not working in your life as you would like, late recovery is a time for restructuring them. This may require some specialized help.

For some recovering persons late recovery poses no serious problems. These persons have come from relatively functional families. From childhood they have developed healthy beliefs and values, and they have learned strategies for coping constructively with life. Their addictions have interfered with their ability to live productively. For these people recovery means rehabilitation, returning to a previous level of health and well being.

Other recovering persons are not so fortunate. They have a great deal of work to do in late recovery because they were raised in dysfunctional or addictive families or because they began using alcohol or drugs at such a young age that emotional growth and development were arrested. They have never learned normal healthy beliefs and attitudes about life and living. Many have developed emotional problems, unrelated to their addictions, that have resulted in the inability to achieve comfort and meaning in sobriety.

In order to resolve issues that go back to your childhood or adolescence, you must first recognize that these issues have created mistaken beliefs that are interfering with comfortable sobriety. These beliefs are forming the basis of self-defeating judgments and decisions. You must carefully analyze-with the help of skilled therapists—the dynamics of the family you grew up in. You need to identify the mistaken beliefs that developed which are now interfering with a meaningful and comfortable sobriety. You must then make decisions to change how you think and act in response to daily challenges and problems. Children Of Alcoholics (COA) support groups are often helpful in this day-to-day change.

The end result of resolving these long-existing issues is freedom from mistaken beliefs that were learned in childhood that have limited the potential for your happiness and satisfaction in recovery. It allows you the opportunity to develop healthy selfesteem that can result in spiritual growth, healthy intimacy, and productive, meaningful living.

The purpose of late recovery is developing belief systems, value systems, and coping skills for full and productive living. When your lifestyle is stabilized, you come to want something more. It can be a dangerous time because your addictive personality will cause you to want an addictive lifestyle. You must recognize that the purpose of life is not to escape reality. When your whole purpose in life was to live life in the fast track, you knew how to get immediate gratification. In order to live a more fulfilled life you need to make changes that may be temporarily painful. During late recovery you look at your purpose for living and make changes in values that will allow you to live a more meaningful life.

LATE RECOVERY: Development of healthy self-esteem, spiritual growth, healthy intimacy, and meaningful living.

THE MAINTENANCE PERIOD

The primary goal of the maintenance period is productive sober living. This involves maintaining an effective recovery program, identifying relapse warning signs, daily problem solving, and productive living. Addiction is a chronic disease that never goes away. As a recovering person you must maintain a sobriety-centered lifestyle that makes managing stress, resolving problems, and maintaining honesty in your personal relationships a priority. You must also maintain an awareness of your addictive potential and carefully avoid addictive chemicals and compulsive behaviors.

MAINTENANCE: Staying sober and living **productively.**

PARTIAL RECOVERY

Recovery from addictive disease is not a process of straight line growth. Most persons recover in stages over time. They develop a new understanding of their disease and recovery. They spend time applying and integrating that new knowledge into their daily lives. They then become comfortable and coast for awhile before the need for new knowledge develops.

It is common for recovering people to temporarily back-slide in their recovery. This often happens when they are attempting to put new knowledge to work. The stress of change temporarily gets the best of them and they back off for awhile. As the stress goes down, they talk about how to better manage the situation, they roll up their sleeves, and they get started again. Many recovering people eventually achieve longterm and comfortable sobriety. (170)

Recovery from addictive disease is not a process of straight line growth.

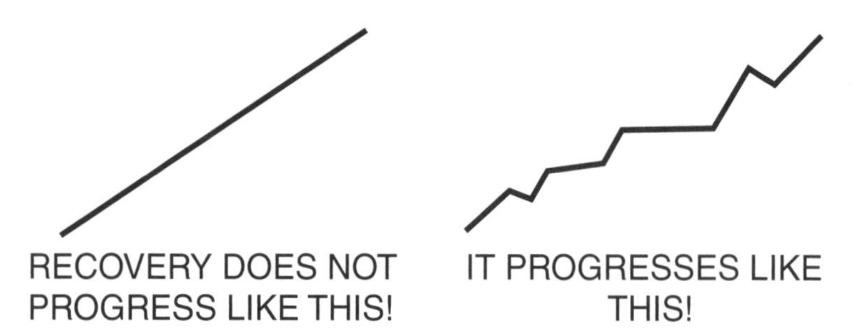

RECOVERY DOES NOT PROGRESS LIKE THIS!

IT PROGRESSES LIKE THIS!

Many recovering people do not make it all the way through the recovery process. Partial recovery begins when they confront a recovery task that they believe to be unmanageable or insurmountable. This insurmountable recovery task is called a "stuck point." Being "stuck" causes them to fail to complete all of the recovery tasks. The consequence is that they remain uncomfortable and experience a low-quality sobriety.

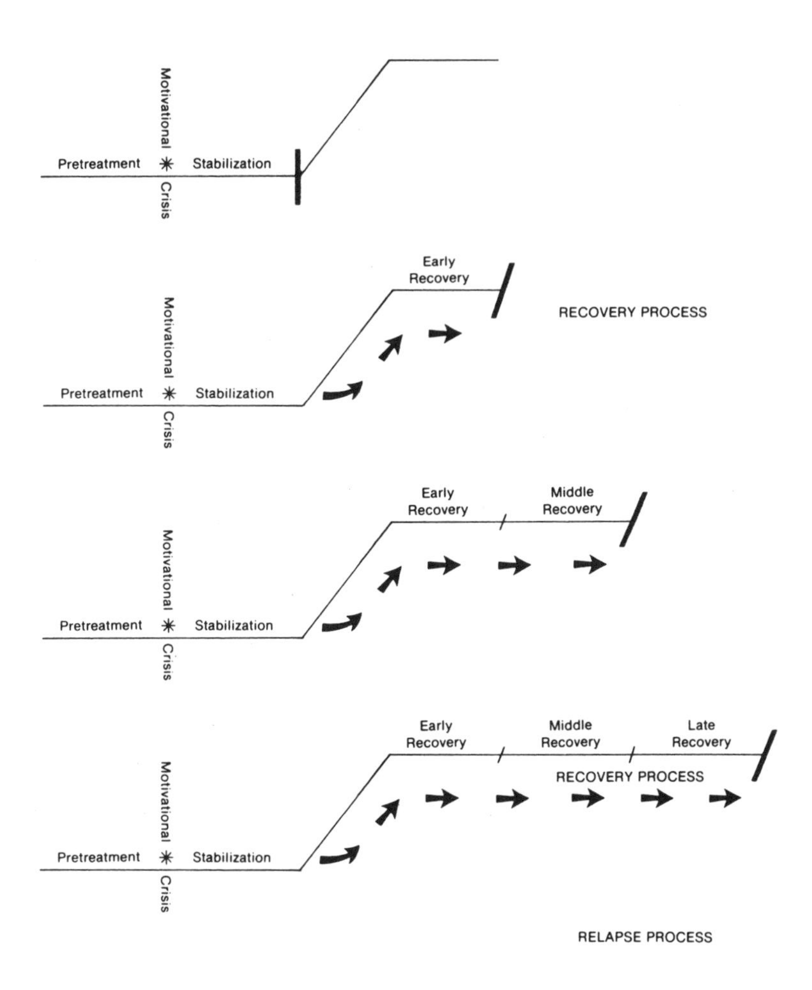

Diagram 2: Stuck Point in Partial Recovery.
A person can experience a stuck point at any place in recovery. The most common stuck point occurs in transition between recovery stages.

A healthy and productive response to hitting a stuck point is to temporarily back off in order to lower stress. The next step is to rationally examine the stuck point by discussing it with other people and then to seek appropriate help in coping with the stuck point.

Instead of taking these productive steps, many people who are stuck in recovery use denial to cope with the stuck point. The denial is not used consciously. They automatically block the awareness that something is wrong. The stuck point produces stress; the denial, while temporarily blocking the awareness of the stress, eventually intensifies it.

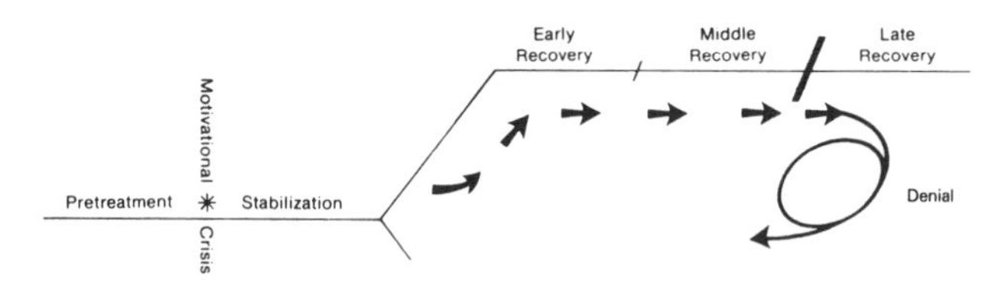

Diagram 3: The Role of Denial in Partial Recovery.
Partial recovery begins when the stuck point is denied. The person says, "My recovery is fine. There is nothing wrong with me."

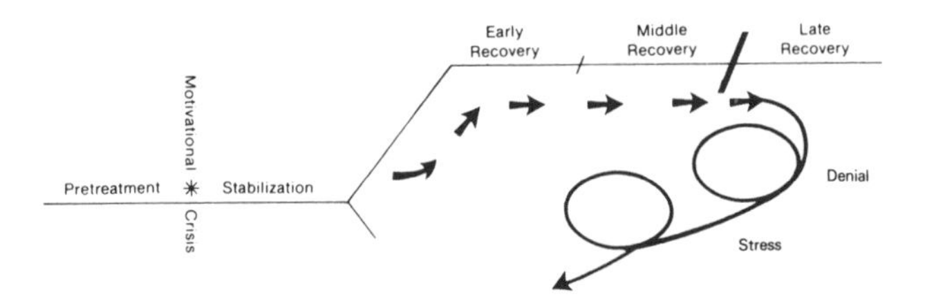

Diagram 4: Stress and Partial Recovery.
The denial of the stuck point produces an increase in stress.

As the stress increases, post acute withdrawal symptoms begin to develop and get worse. This means people develop difficulty in thinking clearly, managing feelings and emotions, remembering things, and recognizing and managing stress. They may also have difficulty sleeping restfully or they may become accident prone. Many recovering people do not consciously recognize the PAW symptoms. This may be because they do not know about PAW. It may also be that stress is blocking their ability to think clearly about themselves. As a result, they cannot manage the PAW symptoms. Instead they attempt to cope with them with more denial. The denial raises the stress; the stress makes the PAW worse. The PAW creates more problems, and these problems create additional stress that further aggravates the PAW.

The original stuck point is often overshadowed by severe problems that result from mismanaging the PAW. A person becomes preoccupied with these problems and fails to identify the primary cause of what is happening.

He or she becomes progressively more stressed. The increased stress leads to a state of free-floating anxiety and compulsion. The person feels compelled to do something, anything, to relieve the anxiety and compulsion, often adopting compulsive behaviors that temporarily relieve the stress. The compulsive behavior, however, produces additional long-term problems in exchange for the short-term relief.

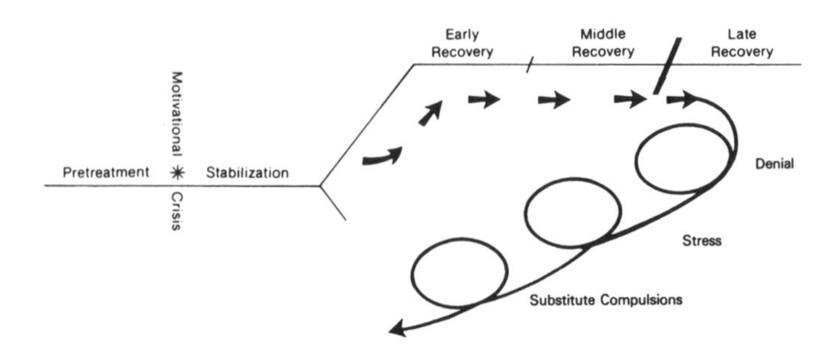

Diagram 5: Substitute Compulsions.
In an effort to cope with the stress, substitute compulsions such as overworking, overeating, overspending, etc. are used. These compulsive behaviors bring short-term relief but increase stress in the long run.

Eventually the stress leads to the activation of the relapse process and these people begin losing control. As the loss of control breaks into conscious awareness, they see the handwriting on the wall. (If they keep doing what they are doing, they will use alcohol or drugs, go crazy, or attempt suicide to turn off the pain.) At this point they often reactivate their recovery programs and life is stabilized. They progress in recovery until the same block is encountered all over again.

As stress increases, post acute withdrawal symptoms begin to develop and get worse.

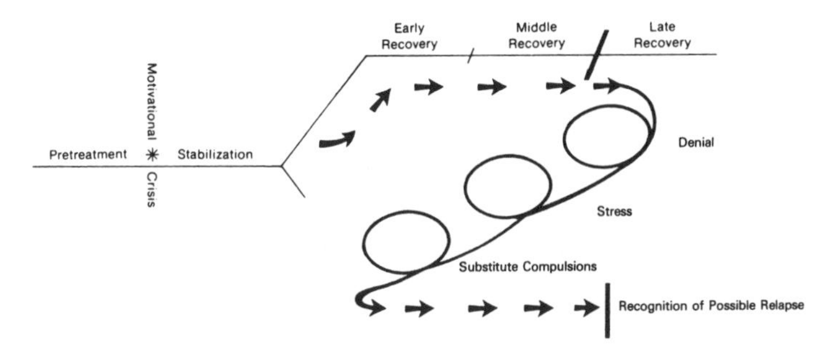

Diagram 6: The Relapse Process.
Eventually the stress becomes so severe that the relapse process, marked by progressive internal and external dysfunction, begins to develop. The person recognizes the risk of relapse.

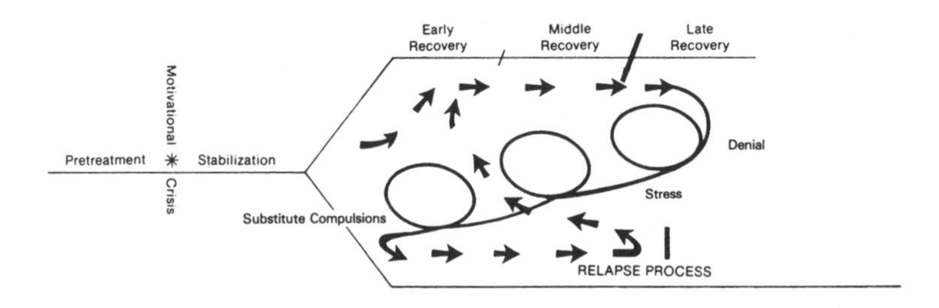

Diagram 7: Repeating the Cycle.
The person reactivates a recovery program and progresses until the same stuck point is reached. The cycle begins again.

It is often easy to believe that this IS recovery. Recovering people can become locked into a pattern of partial recovery. They progress repeatedly to the same point where they again, unknowingly, begin the relapse process. Eventually, they recognize the progressive loss of control that precedes an acute relapse episode. The fear of relapse motivates them to take some action to put themselves back into the recovery process, but they return once again to the first stage of recovery where they are comfortable. They pursue an active recovery program until they again encounter a stage that they perceive as too frightening to face, and the cycle of partial recovery continues. They may repeat the same pattern over and over. The BIG BOOK of AA calls it "half measures."

Joan is a 57-year-old alcoholic. She has been sober for 16 years with AA. When she stopped drinking she was told to make 90 meetings in 90 days. It worked so well that she never saw any reason to change that pattern. Joan is married to a man she does not really love but feels obligated to because of her religion. She works full time as a secretary in a large hospital. She feels that she is capable of being an administrative assistant, but that her promotions are blocked because others take credit for her accomplishments.

When she gets upset about her marriage or her job, she goes to AA meetings, talks with her sponsor, and then does her best to turn the problems over by forcing them out of her mind. Her recovery is a roller coaster ride. At times she feels excited or serene and thanks her Higher Power for recovery, but at other times she feels so much pain and frustration that she thinks she might die.

The cycle is predictable. Over a period of three to five months Joan gets more and more depressed and anxious until finally she starts thinking about drinking or using tranquilizers to reduce the pain. She talks to her sponsor and comments at meetings about her pain and her desire to drink, but she never talks to anyone about the problems causing the pain.

When she thinks about drinking she doubles her AA attendance, sometimes attending two or three meetings a day. Then as she reduces her meeting attendance and becomes reinvolved in her marriage and job the pain comes back and she starts thinking about drinking.

Joan hasn't had a drink in 16 years, but she finds little more than temporary escape from the ongoing pain of a dysfunctional recovery. The quality of her sobriety could be greatly improved if she recognized her need to resolve ongoing life problems that periodically cause her to think about drinking.

Some people who experience partial recovery do not recognize the progressive loss of control that accompanies the relapse syndrome. Their lives become out of control even though they may be outwardly pursuing a recovery program. Believing that attendance at AA meetings or an aftercare group alone will ensure continued sobriety, they relapse. And they, as well as those close to them, wonder what happened.

Partial recovery is not sobriety.

It is not all right to waste your life in partial recovery. You are worth more than that. There is something better than that. The consequence of partial recovery is living a life of low-grade crisis, pain, and discomfort. Stress of partial recovery can and does cause stress-related illnesses that can and do shorten life. You CAN recognize the stuck points and move beyond them into full recovery.

Chapter V

MISTAKEN BELIEFS ABOUT RECOVERY AND RELAPSE

The first step in preventing relapse is to understand what it is and what it is not. The more you know and understand about relapse the less risk there is that you will experience it and the less threatening it will be for you.

There are a great many mistaken beliefs that trap relapse prone persons into a state of hopelessness. Many people have these mistaken beliefs and act as if they are true.

Mistaken beliefs about relapse create self-fulfilling prophecies. When mistaken beliefs become "truth" to you, you ACT as if those beliefs are true.

The problem with mistaken beliefs is that they prevent the effective problem solving needed to interrupt the cycle of relapse. Mistaken beliefs about relapse create self-fulfilling prophecies. When mistaken beliefs become "truth" to you, you ACT as if those beliefs are true. These inappropriate behaviors lead you into a relapse cycle so that the mistaken belief you have becomes real.

We would like to dispel some of the myths and mistaken notions about relapse and replace them with factual knowledge that will help you to deal more realistically with the relapse potential of your illness.

The mistaken beliefs that prevent relapse prone people from recovering fall into four areas. These areas are:

1. Mistaken beliefs about the role of alcohol and drug use in recovery and relapse.
2. Mistaken beliefs about the presence and nature of relapse warning signs.
3. Mistaken beliefs about the meaning and role of motivation in recovery.
4. Mistaken beliefs about the effectiveness of treatment.

Each of these will be reviewed in detail to show how a combination of mistaken beliefs can lead to a series of erroneous conclusions that create a self-defeating cycle of chronic relapse.

MISTAKEN BELIEFS ABOUT THE ROLE OF ALCOHOL AND DRUG USE IN RECOVERY

Many relapse prone people believe that recovery is abstinence from alcohol and drug use and that relapse is the use of alcohol and drugs. This leads them to believe that anytime they abstain from alcohol and drugs they are in recovery and anytime they return to alcohol and drug use they are in relapse. As a result, they come to believe that not using alcohol and drugs is their primary task in recovery.

Recovery is not abstinence from alcohol and drug use. Abstinence is only a prerequisite for recovery. The actual recovery process involves completing a series of tasks daily that allow management of acute and post acute withdrawal and the correction of the bio-psycho-social damage caused by the addiction. In other words, recovery is a lot more than simply not using alcohol and drugs. If you believe that simply not using will produce recovery, you will be surprised at the dysfunction caused by the sobriety-based symptoms of addiction. You may also feel trapped and helpless because your mistaken beliefs keep you from finding a way to deal with these symptoms.

Many relapse prone alcoholics extend mistaken beliefs even further. If you believe that recovery is abstinence from alcohol and drug use then you come to believe that as long as you do not use alcohol or drugs you will be in control of yourself and your behavior. You mistakenly believe that when you are sober you are always in control. The only way to lose control is to use alcohol and drugs. This leads to the conclusion that any return to alcohol and drug use must be a conscious and willful decision. Relapse, therefore, is a conscious and deliberate choice. It is assumed that as long as you choose not to use alcohol and drugs you will maintain control and be fine.

Let us review this sequence of mistaken beliefs:

1. Recovery is abstinence from alcohol and drugs.
2. Relapse is alcohol and drug use.

3. Anytime I abstain from alcohol and drugs I am in recovery.
4. Anytime I return to alcohol and drug use I am in relapse.
5. As long as I don't use alcohol and drugs I will be in control of myself and my behavior.
   Conclusion: Relapse is always the result of a conscious and deliberate choice to use alcohol and drugs.
   Conclusion: Not using alcohol and drugs is my primary task in recovery.

The error is that not using alcohol and drugs does not guarantee that you will be in control of yourself and automatically recover. Not using alcohol and drugs will break the addiction cycle and stop episodes of loss of control caused by intoxication. But, as we discussed earlier, when the alcohol/drug based symptoms are interrupted by abstinence, they are replaced by sobriety-based symptoms. These sobriety-based symptoms can be so severe that they cause you to lose control of your judgment and behavior even when sober.

Many alcoholics who relapse report that they became so dysfunctional in recovery that a return to addictive use seemed like a positive option. They were in so much pain that they came to believe they only had three choices left: (1) alcohol and drug use to medicate pain, (2) suicide, or (3) insanity. Given these options, the alcohol and drug use seemed like the best choice.

Abstinence from alcohol and drug use is necessary for recovery but is not the only goal in recovery. Learning how to live a meaningful and comfortable life without alcohol or drug use is the primary goal of recovery.

Sobriety-based symptoms—including short-term and long-term withdrawal, the inability to cope with life without alcohol and drugs, and the crisis created by the bio-psycho-social damage of addiction—will interfere with the ability to have a comfortable and meaningful life without alcohol and drugs. In order to recover it is important to stop using alcohol and other mood-altering drugs and then to learn how to cope with withdrawal and the stress of life without returning to the use of alcohol and drugs.

Abstinence is not the only goal of recovery.

MISTAKEN BELIEFS ABOUT THE WARNING SIGNS OF RELAPSE

A common mistaken belief is that relapse just suddenly and spontaneously occurs without warning signs. This belief produces a feeling of helplessness and powerlessness. Relapse remains a mysterious process over which recovering persons have little or no control. All they can do is hope and pray that relapse does not occur.

Relapse does not occur suddenly and spontaneously without warning.

The truth is that there are many warning signs that precede a relapse. Once you learn to recognize and manage the early warning signs of relapse you can stop the relapse process before it has a chance to get started. If you are locked into the mistaken belief that relapse is alcohol and drug use, you will be able to identify only a very few relapse warning signs.

People who believe that relapse is only alcohol or drug use will only identify warning signs that relate to drinking or using drugs. These warning signs are typically:

—thinking about alcohol and drug use,

—developing a compulsion to use alcohol or drugs,

—placing oneself in situations where others are drinking or using drugs,

—stopping attendance at self-help groups or other recovery activities.

These people believe that they will always know when they are experiencing the warning signs. They fail to recognize that denial carries over into sobriety and can block the recognition of these warning signs.

The final step in this erroneous reasoning process goes something like this: "Once I am aware of the warning signs, I will always be capable of coping with them if I want to." Let's review these mistaken beliefs:

1. All warning signs relate to drinking or drug use or missing AA meetings.
2. I will always know it when I am experiencing these relapse warning signs.
3. Once I am aware of the warning signs I will always be able to cope with them if I want to.

Conclusion: As long as I am not thinking about using and I am going to meetings I am fine.

The problem with these beliefs is very serious. Thinking about alcohol and drug use, feeling a compulsion to use, placing oneself in situations of alcohol and drug use, and stopping recovery activities ARE serious relapse warning signs. But these warning signs occur very late in the relapse process. By the time these warning signs develop, many alcoholics are already out of control of their judgment and behavior. As a result, they may be unable to recognize or take action to interrupt these warning signs.

MISTAKEN BELIEFS ABOUT MOTIVATION

Most recovering persons observe the fact that relapse is a relatively frequent occurrence. As a result, they must develop some ways to explain why. Given the preceding mistaken beliefs, many recovering persons develop the following erroneous beliefs:

1. If I relapse I am not motivated to recover.
2. I will recover when I hurt enough as a result of my alcohol and drug use to want to recover.

3. If I relapse I have not hurt enough to want to stay sober.

   Conclusion: Relapse prone people need to hurt more in order to interrupt their relapse patterns.

This is a devastating conclusion for relapse prone persons to reach. It may cause you to question your sanity if you know that you want to get well but are unable to do it. This destroys self-worth and self-esteem and produces shame and guilt.

It is true that some chemically dependent people relapse because they do not believe they are alcoholic. And they have not accepted their alcoholism because they have not developed consequences severe enough to convince themselves. But this relapse pattern only applies to persons in the pretreatment period of recovery. It does not apply to relapse prone people who know they are addicted and that they cannot safely use alcohol or drugs. And yet they cannot stay sober no matter how hard they try.

Most relapse prone alcoholics are in terrible pain. In fact, the pain is so severe that it prevents them from functioning when sober. The severe pain actually prevents them from benefitting from their recovery program.

Pain does not prevent relapse; it may increase the risk.

MISTAKEN BELIEFS ABOUT TREATMENT

Many persons who are recovering from addictive disease work very hard to recover. They attend counseling and group therapy. They regularly attend 12-step, self-help groups. Yet they fail to recover.

These people develop one of two equally destructive mistaken beliefs. The first mistaken belief is that no form of treatment or self-help group can work. This simply is not true. There are many documented cases of relapse prone patients who recovered after going back and reapplying themselves to recovery programs that had not worked before. Another attempt at treatment or AA is always worth the risk.

An equally destructive belief is the complete opposite. This is the belief that treatment (AA plus professional counseling) is 100% effective for anyone who wants to recover and that the major cause of relapse is the decision to drop out of treatment. With this belief, when people fail at treatment they assume that it is because there is something inherently wrong with them that makes it impossible to recover.

Let's look at these mistaken beliefs:

1. No form of treatment or self-help group can help me stay sober.
2. Treatment is 100% effective in preventing relapse.

   Conclusion: If I relapse it is because I am constitutionally incapable of recovery.

   Conclusion: There is no point in getting additional treatment; I cannot get well.

The fact is that there is good treatment and bad treatment. There is treatment that is effective for some but not for others. And there is much that is still unknown about what is effective treatment for addictive disease. Some people relapse because they have not attained the skills to stay sober. But that does not mean that they cannot. Treatment appears to be 20–60% successful dependent upon how you measure success. (190) (193) (201) (72) (204) (189)

A history of relapse is by no means a sign that you cannot recover. It is not an indication that you are constitutionally incapable of recovery. It is an indication that you are a pretty typical alcoholic or chemically dependent person and that you need to roll up your sleeves and get back into treatment. Chances are good that if you find a program that uses relapse prevention planning, you will be able to achieve long-term sobriety or at least learn to stay sober for longer periods of time and significantly improve your life. The purpose of this book is to show you how, with accurate information, to begin doing just that.

Chances are good that with relapse prevention planning you can achieve long-term sobriety.

Chapter VI

UNDERSTANDING THE RELAPSE PROCESS

What is relapse? This question is not as easy to answer as it appears at first. To get an accurate answer let us examine how the concept of relapse developed historically.

In the early days of AA, in the mid 1930s, alcoholics were considered to have relapsed only when they began drinking again. Relapse was defined simply as a return to alcohol use. As alcoholics started substituting drug use for drinking, they became aware that alcoholics cannot safely use any sedative drugs. Alcohol is a sedative drug and it is now known that any sedative drug has an effect on the body similar to alcohol. In fact, some professional people have begun using the term "sedativism" instead of "alcoholism" because it is not the alcohol that is the problem but the reaction of the body to sedative drugs. So relapse came to mean use of any sedative drugs (including alcohol).

With the common use of a variety of drugs in the '60s some people began to be aware that any type of mood-altering drug could trigger relapse. Drugs such as amphetamines, marijuana, cocaine, or LSD have an effect on the body that is different from the effect of sedative drugs. But they still change the mental and emotional state and impair judgment so that a person begins to move away from recovery. They have the same behavioral effect in that they cause you to feel good now, cause pain later, and induce obsession, compulsion, and loss of control. Abusing any drug or combination of drugs will also eventually cause bio-psycho-social damage. It became clear that any mood-altering drug can reactivate the addiction cycle. As a result of this new knowledge alcoholics began to think of relapse as use of any mood-altering chemical (remember that alcohol is a mood-altering drug).

Understanding of what "relapse" is has changed from
—ALCOHOL USE to
—USE OF ANY SEDATIVE DRUG to
—USE OF ANY MOOD-ALTERING DRUG.

While thinking of relapse as a return to alcohol or drug use, professional treatment providers and members of AA have always recognized that it takes more than just not using alcohol and drugs to recover. Only the first step of AA mentions alcohol. The other steps talk about how to live sober. Instead of focusing on "not drinking," the focus is on learning how to live effectively and comfortably without addictive use. This leads us to the concept that relapse has as much to do with how an individual is functioning as it does with whether or not that person is using alcohol or drugs. Not using alcohol or drugs is a prerequisite for recovery, but recovery involves much more than simply not using.

With this way of thinking, the process of relapse includes becoming dysfunctional in sobriety. This dysfunction may involve physical, psychological, or social health. This does not mean that addictive use is not relapse. It means that the process of relapse is occurring before addictive use begins! When addictive use starts, it is a RESULT of the relapse process that is already occurring. Addictive use is a way to medicate the pain of the dysfunction. The dysfunction begins as a mental process that in AA is called "stinking thinking." That leads to a change in behavior that AA calls a "setup." It finally leads to dysfunctional behavior in sobriety that in AA is called a "dry drunk." This dry drunk may lead to addictive use or some other form of serious dysfunction such as emotional disturbance, physical collapse, or stress-related illness.

Many recovering alcoholics have remained drug free but have committed suicide or have collapsed physically or emotionally. This is not recovery. The concept of the relapse process as drinking or drug use only, prevents treatment of sobriety-based symptoms of addiction. Many sobriety-based symptoms of alcoholism and chemical dependence have been ignored or misinterpreted as psychological or psychiatric problems. Depression, confusion, and anxiety that emerge as symptoms of acute and post acute withdrawal are often not recognized as symptoms of the addiction. So appropriate treatment for them is not sought or offered or encouraged. Many recovering people suffering from these addiction-related problems are referred to psychologists or psychiatrists who know little or nothing about the addictive disease that is causing the problem.

With this expanded understanding of the process of relapse, the focus of life is not just on using or not using. It is on recovery from damage caused by the addiction, on learning to manage sobriety-based symptoms, and on improving bio-psycho-social health. This allows life to be centered around healthful living, not around alcohol and drugs.

This encourages you to learn about and recognize the early warning signs of relapse before you are forced to begin addictive use in an effort to make those symptoms go away. If addictive use is the only indicator of relapse, then as long as you are abstinent you believe you are fine. You are not concerned about other situations in your life that might be as serious as drinking. Neglect of these other important life areas can be very harmful to your recovery.

THE ROLE OF SUBSTITUTE ADDICTIONS

Once a person becomes addicted or dependent upon one drug there is a tendency to transfer that dependency to other mood-altering drugs. This is especially true if the other drug is similar to the original drug of dependency. This process is called cross addiction. To become addicted to one drug will cause rapid addiction to any other drug in that group. The reason is primarily physical. The body becomes dependent upon that type of drug and will respond in the same way to drugs that are similar.

A person can also become dependent upon mood-altering drugs from different drug groups. This dependency to the new drug develops gradually.

A person can transfer dependencies to a variety of other drugs. This process can be best understood by looking at what is called the addiction equation:

PAIN + ALCOHOL/DRUGS =
IMMEDIATE PLEASURE + FUTURE PAIN

Chemically dependent people have come to rely on a primary drug of choice to cope with life. If, when they abstain from that drug, they merely substitute a new drug they can develop a dependency on the new drug.

The substitute drug may not be as effective as the primary drug of choice in relieving the pain. This causes these people to think about and crave the original drug. Also, during periods of intoxication their judgment may be impaired causing them to make an irresponsible choice to use the primary drug again.

Changing from one addiction to another is not full recovery. If you believe that you can safely use large amounts of nicotine and caffeine, smoke marijuana, use diet pills or over-the-counter sleep aids as long as you are not using alcohol or other drugs, you are in high risk of developing a second addiction.

It is true that some addictions are more harmful than others. And some chemical addictions, such as to alcohol, cocaine, or heroin, are more dangerous than addiction to caffeine or nicotine. In most cases caffeine addiction will not cause the same type of severe problems that result from alcohol or marijuana addiction. And some people can continue the use of caffeine and nicotine without increasing the amount. But the truth is that the addictive use of caffeine and nicotine can be lethal. The American Cancer Society reports that more people die from cancer caused by nicotine addiction than by abuse of any other drug.

THE ROLE OF CAFFEINE

In the last few years research has begun to show that caffeine can be used addictively, is harmful to health and functioning, and can reactivate the addictive cycle for people seeking to recover from alcohol addiction. (94) John Blattner has done extensive research into the relationship between caffeine use and recovery. (96) His findings are convincing. Alcoholics tend to be heavier consumers of caffeine than nonalcoholics. Recovering alcoholics who are heavy caffeine users report increased symptoms of physical stress and anxiety when using caffeine. They also report headaches, severe irritability, and emotional overreaction when not using caffeine. These symptoms are part of caffeine withdrawal.

The most important aspect of Blattner's research is the fact that there is an increased tendency toward relapse reported in heavy caffeine users. Caffeine seems to contribute to relapse in the following way: Heavy caffeine users suffer from caffeine-related anxiety, stress, irritability, and overreaction. They do not know that these symptoms are caused by caffeine, so they fear something more serious may be happening to them. The overreaction causes situational problems and also prevents them from coping rationally with the problems as they develop. The end result is increased problems, anger, and frustration that increase the risk of relapse.

As the relationship between heavy caffeine use and relapse is becoming more well known, our understanding of what a "mood-altering drug" is has expanded to include drugs such as caffeine and nicotine that were previously considered harmless to recovery.

THE ROLE OF COMPULSIVE BEHAVIOR IN RELAPSE

Compulsive behaviors are actions that produce intense excitement or emotional release and are followed by long-term pain or discomfort. These behaviors can be internal (thinking, imagining, feeling) or external (working, playing, talking, etc.). Compulsive behaviors make you feel good in the short run but weaken you in the long run.

Many persons who are recovering from alcoholism or drug dependence attempt to substitute compulsive behaviors for the use of addictive drugs. For some, the result is the development of severe compulsive behavior that can interfere with recovery.

Remember the addictive equation: PAIN + ALCOHOL/DRUGS = IMMEDIATE PLEASURE + FUTURE PAIN. When a person comes to rely upon compulsive behaviors as a substitute for alcohol or drugs the equation changes to this: PAIN + COMPULSIVE BE-HAVIOR = IMMEDIATE PLEASURE + FUTURE PAIN. The equation is identical except for the fact that compulsive behavior is substituted for alcohol and drugs.

We are going to group the major compulsive behaviors into eight types.

1. ***Eating/Dieting***—This includes compulsive overeating, compulsive dieting (often called anorexia), and the combination of compulsive binge eating followed by compulsive dieting or vomiting (often called bulimia).
2. ***Gambling***—The compulsive need to risk.
3. ***Working/Achieving***—The compulsive need to keep busy or to accomplish things or excel at everything you do.
4. ***Exercising***—The compulsive need to stimulate the body through physical exertion.
5. ***Sex***—The compulsive need to have sexual experiences.

6. ***Thrill Seeking***—The compulsive need to experience intense stress or thrills.
7. ***Escape***—The compulsive need to avoid the daily routines of life.
8. ***Spending***—The compulsive need to buy or acquire possessions.

COMPULSIVE BEHAVIORS

1. Eating/Dieting
2. Gambling
3. Working/Achieving
4. Exercise
5. Sex
6. Thrill Seeking
7. Escape
8. Spending

Dave nearly lost his family because of his marijuana use, and he did lose them because of his compulsive running. He went into treatment for his marijuana addiction when his wife and children moved out. They agreed to come back when he agreed to get treatment. As part of his recovery program he began running. He set a goal of running three miles a day three days a week and soon attained his goal But he was not satisfied. He began running every day—before work, during his lunch hour, and after work. His family, expecting him to enter into family life now that he was sober, were disappointed to discover that he was seldom around. He was entering races and going from place to place for the competition. On days that he did not run he was restless and irritable.

His wife didn't appreciate his regular comment, "Well, at least I'm sober." She decided that this type of sobriety didn't give her much more of a husband than she had before and she left. This is an example of how other compulsions can cause problems in the same way that chemical addictions can.

POSITIVE OUTLETS VERSUS COMPULSIVE BEHAVIORS

The same behavior can be used compulsively or noncompulsively. Compulsive behavior is not measured so much by what you do as it is by how you do it. Every behavior that can be used compulsively, can be productive if used in a way that does not result in long-term pain or dysfunction.

There is a difference between a compulsive behavior and A POSITIVE OUTLET. A positive outlet is an activity that provides pain-free pleasure. In other words, it feels good now without creating pain later. Healthful exercise, for example, is a positive outlet. It allows an enjoyable and pleasant release of energy. But it is done rationally and noncompulsively. As a result, it does not create problems in the future.

Healthy sex is also a positive outlet. Sexual expression between people who love and care about each other and that is performed in a safe, responsible manner is a joy and asset to both partners. It is noncompulsive, is enhancing for both partners, is a free choice of both partners, and happens in a context where negative consequences are unlikely.

Each compulsive behavior has parallel behaviors that if performed noncompulsively and moderately can form a positive outlet. When a behavior is used compulsively, it is used as some people use drugs. The goal is to alter mood, turn off the mind, and evade reality. The behavior becomes compulsive when it is used to cope with the pain of reality. Behaviors are positive outlets when they enhance reality and help a person to more effectively cope with reality.

If a person is to achieve a high-quality sobriety and avoid relapse it is advisable to abstain from compulsive behaviors and to identify and practice a number of positive outlets that give pain-free pleasure.

Some alcoholics and drug dependent persons have developed serious problems with compulsive behaviors. Attempting to stop the compulsive behavior produces pain and feels like withdrawal. If this happens to you, you will need special help to stop the compulsive behavior. You actually have two problems: chemical dependency and a compulsive behavior problem. Don't be afraid to get help for it. It can make your sobriety much more comfortable and help you to avoid relapse.

Compulsive behavior is not what you do but how you do it.

THE PROCESS OF RELAPSE

The tendency to ignore other symptoms of relapse, cross addiction to "acceptable drugs" like nicotine and caffeine, and the use of compulsive behaviors allows the PROCESS of relapse (dysfunction in sobriety) to begin. When you begin the process of dysfunction, you begin the process of relapse. Looking at the process of relapse you recognize that there are warning signs before an acute relapse episode occurs. When you recognize relapse warning signs before you drink, you can get help and interrupt the process.

Sobriety is abstinence from addictive drugs plus abstinence from compulsive behaviors plus improvements in bio-psycho-social health. Sobriety includes all three things. To the extent that you have accomplished those three things you are sober; to the extent that you have not accomplished those three things you are not sober. It is not defined entirely by whether or not you are drinking or using drugs. It is defined by the completeness of your sobriety.

SOBRIETY IS

Abstinence from addictive drugs +
Abstinence from compulsive behaviors +
Improvements in bio/psycho/social health.

Relapse Prevention Planning is based upon the fact that the symptoms of the addictive disease do not stop with abstinence. This is a disease that has two cutting edges. The first attacks while you are drinking or using. This is the obvious side of the disease. What is not so obvious is that the disease extends into abstinence and takes a vicious toll while you are attempting to recover. This sobriety-based side of the disease is as powerful and destructive as the alcohol/drug-based side. And you are even more helpless when it occurs because it is generally misunderstood and unrecognized.

It is the sobriety-based symptoms of addiction that lead to relapse.

SOBRIETY-BASED DENIAL

It is very easy to take denial into recovery. Even if you have acknowledged your addiction and you have stopped using, you are used to thinking in a way that supports what you want to believe. It is easier to say, "Everything is all right now that I have quit drinking" than it is to admit that you need to carefully follow a recovery program for the rest of your life.

When it is uncomfortable or threatening to see things as they are, it is easy to blank them out or to alter them in your mind so they seem less threatening. Filtering out painful information is a way of coping that can bring short-term relief but bring about more intense pain in the long run. The trade off for inaccurate awareness is an immediate sense of security. You can cope with painful reality by pushing it from your conscious awareness, but there is a price. That price could be relapse.

There are certain circumstances and conditions that can set you up for making bad decisions about your recovery. These situations can lead to relapse if you allow denial, self-deceptive thinking, and lack of accurate information to cloud your understanding of what you need to do to progress in recovery.

There are signs along the way that the relapse process is occurring. If it is uncomfortable or threatening to acknowledge these warning signs, it is easy to blank them out of conscious awareness or to "twist" them into a more acceptable reality. That will help you be more secure and comfortable now. But it will allow the relapse process to continue and to gather momentum until it is out of control.

The symptoms of relapse usually develop on a ***subconscious level***. Because they are out of your conscious awareness, the symptoms are allowed to build and to intensify. You are not consciously aware of them until they are out of control. When your perceptions, your judgment, and your behavior are out of control, you will probably be unable to interrupt the relapse process before it results in an acute relapse episode.

While relapse is a very real possibility, it can be avoided. Through the process of relapse prevention planning, you can learn ways to manage the sobrietybased symptoms and bring them into conscious awareness before it is too late. You can learn to interrupt the relapse process before you become dysfunctional.

You can learn from the past. As a matter of fact, the past is your best and most effective teacher. It teaches you what works and what does not work. By allowing the past to teach you how to stay sober, you can avoid addictive use in the future. And you can avoid other types of dysfunction such as an emotional or physical collapse.

There are predictable and progressive warning signs that occur in most recovering persons before a return to addictive use. The warning signs will begin with minor changes in thinking and behavior. You will convince yourself that your addiction is no longer a priority issue. Other things become more important. You will then begin to use old behaviors instead of the new behaviors you have learned and made part of your recovery program. The old behaviors trigger old problems and the use of old denial patterns. These changes increase your discomfort and make a return to using not only possible but desirable. But you will probably not be consciously aware of the changes that have taken place in your thinking and in your behavior.

Relapse Prevention Planning teaches you how to become aware of these changes and to choose positive alternatives to addictive chemicals and compulsive behaviors and alternatives to continued isolation, avoidance, and denial. You can interrupt this pattern at any point if you learn how.

Before you are in trouble you should design a plan that will allow your family, your friends, your counselor, and self-help group members to help you interrupt a potential or an actual relapse episode should it occur. You should make some rules that you want others to follow to help you avoid the destructive consequences of relapse. Relapse Prevention Planning is the process of bringing symptoms of relapse into conscious awareness and taking action that will allow you to remove them from your life.

Chapter VII

THE RELAPSE SYNDROME

Recovery from addiction must be an active process. Recovering persons must work a daily program of recovery. They must remind themselves daily that they are suffering from an addiction. They must have an active recovery program that provides guidelines for effective and productive living.

Recovery is like walking up a down escalator. It is impossible to stand still.

Recovery from addiction is like walking up a down escalator. It is impossible to stand still. When you stop moving forward, you find yourself moving backwards. You do not have to do anything in particular to develop symptoms that lead to relapse. All you need to do is to fail to take appropriate recovery steps. The symptoms develop spontaneously in the absence of a strong recovery program.* Once you abandon a recovery program it is only a matter of time until the symptoms of post acute withdrawal appear, and if nothing is done to manage them, you will experience a period of out-of-control behavior that we call the relapse syndrome. Loss of control of post acute withdrawal symptoms results in the relapse syndrome.

*There have been many studies and articles on the process of relapse. (See references in bibliography under RELAPSE.)

Post acute withdrawal symptoms are experienced by most recovering persons, but they vary in severity. It is how they are managed that determines the severity of the relapse syndrome.

Relapse Syndrome = PAW - Symptom Management

If you are experiencing PAW and you do not do whatever is necessary to effectively manage those symptoms, the relapse syndrome will eventually take over. The symptoms will build, grow, and progress. There are many subtle warning signs and many changes in thoughts, emotions, and personality that occur before loss of control. Eventually you will lose control of yourself. You will begin going down a progression that will lead to alcohol or drug use or to some other acute emotional or physical reaction unless something is done to interrupt that progression.

It is important for you to always be aware that the relapse process does not only involve the act of taking a drink or using drugs. It is a progression that creates the overwhelming need for alcohol or drugs. It is this progression that we call the relapse syndrome.

It is possible to interrupt this progression before the warning signs are obvious. If nothing is done until you are showing the obvious signs it is usually very difficult to interrupt the relapse syndrome because you have already lost control of your judgment and your behavior. Relapse is not usually a conscious choice. Studies have shown that relapsing people are generally not consciously aware of the early warning signs of their relapse. Later, when they look back, they can identify what went wrong, but at the time it was happening they were unaware that these problems were building and growing. The signs of relapse develop on an unconscious level. You will not know they are occurring unless you learn to bring the warning signs into conscious awareness.

The relapse process does not only involve the act of taking a drink or using drugs. It is a progression that creates the overwhelming need for alcohol or drugs.

This progression can occur easily without an effective recovery program and without effective management of the symptoms of PAW. The process usually begins with **change**. Change is a normal part of life but a major cause of stress. The change may be an external event that forces you to respond in some way. Or it can be a change in thinking or attitude.

Change produces **stress** to which you are apt to overreact and for which you probably have low tolerance. As stress levels are elevated, there is a normal tendency to deny the presence of stress and trigger ***denial*** mechanisms that are part of addictive disease. You begin to deal with stress with the same kind of ***denial*** you once used to justify using. "I don't have a problem. I can handle it. Everything is all right."

The elevated stress intensifies the symptoms of ***post acute withdrawal***, but your denial will keep you from seeing what is happening. If nothing is done, the PAW symptoms will increase. You lose control of your thinking, your emotions, and your memory. You do not think clearly, you overreact, you cannot remember simple things. Stress intensifies. You lose control of your ability to think, to feel, and to remember.

Then you lose control of your behavior. You may go to the same places and engage in the same activities, but you experience a ***behavior change***. You do not act the same. You treat people differently. You interact in a different way and there is a ***breakdown in social structure***.

In fact, all ***life structure breaks down***. You change your daily routine. You abandon regular habits that give your life consistency and dependability. Your recovery plans are neglected and avoided.

Eventually you ***lose control of judgment***. You make bad choices that in a normal state of mind you would never make. As a result, you make mistakes and create a crisis. Your life has become unmanageable. You are ***out of control***. You are able to see that you are no longer in control of your life. You believe you may be going crazy. You see no alternatives to going crazy other than killing yourself or using alcohol or drugs to medicate the pain. You think there are ***no other options.***

At this point you are in a state of ***acute degeneration***. Your life is falling apart. You may return to using because it seems better than the other alternatives. But not everyone who experiences the relapse syndrome uses. Some experience an equally destructive alternative. Some commit suicide or injure themselves in serious accidents. Others have nervous breakdowns or physical or emotional collapse. Others develop stress-related illnesses such as migraine headaches, ulcers, or hypertension.

It is possible to interrupt the relapse progression before the warning signs are obvious.

Kenneth was a 47-year-old man who was married with two teenage children. He had seven years of abstinence. He had a firm conviction that he would never drink again even if it killed him. He had worked for the same railroad for 17 years.

For several years Kenneth had worked the night shift and had enjoyed having less supervision at work and his days free to do odd jobs for extra cash. Because of manpower cutbacks he was changed to the day shift.

The shift change created a lot of stress for Kenneth because he had trouble sleeping when he was used to being awake and there were financial problems caused by giving up his extra jobs. In addition, he was around his family more and it was difficult to get used to the children's noise.

When people close to him noticed that he seemed more uptight than usual, Kenneth repeatedly told them, "I am going to be okay. I just need time to adjust."

Before long Kenneth began to feel like the children were deliberately making noise to irritate him. It seemed that his wife picked fights and his mind always seemed clouded and confused. Making even little decisions was difficult.

Kenneth didn't like the people at the evening AA meetings as much as those at the noon meetings so it became easier to skip meetings. Although usually quick to call a friend to share a joke, the calls and the jokes came less and less frequently. It seemed that it didn't take anything to "set him off" and to trigger his verbal abuse.

Kenneth's kids began to be around less and less when he was home. His wife withdrew and confided in her sponsor that she didn't know how much longer she could stand this.

Finally Kenneth's AA attendance stopped altogether. He no longer met his buddies at the cafe for coffee, and they didn't go out to dinner with friends. He seldom ate with the family and began snacking rather than having regular meals.

Because of his financial frustration Kenneth sold his good truck and bought one much older that cost twice as much to maintain. He decided to have the driveway repaved rather than have the washer and TV repaired. His bad judgment just made his financial problems worse and created other life problems. He began to oversleep and call in sick rather than go to work.

Kenneth's wife reached the point that she was threatening divorce, his job had given him two verbal and one written warning, and his son had moved in with a friend to avoid the hassle.

Still firmly committed to not drinking, Kenneth began to plan his suicide. "If I just make it look like I fell under the train...."

Kenneth's wife became aware that relapse can be interrupted and gave him the choice of treatment or divorce. He chose treatment. He chose life instead of suicide. He sought treatment for his relapse even though he had not taken a drink.

The relapse syndrome is the sobriety-based disease of addiction.

The relapse syndrome can destroy your health and well-being; it can destroy your family and your lifestyle. It is the sobriety-based disease of addiction, and it can be devastating to the recovering person.

Many recovering people believe that if they are not using, their recovery is fine. This is a mistake. The relapse

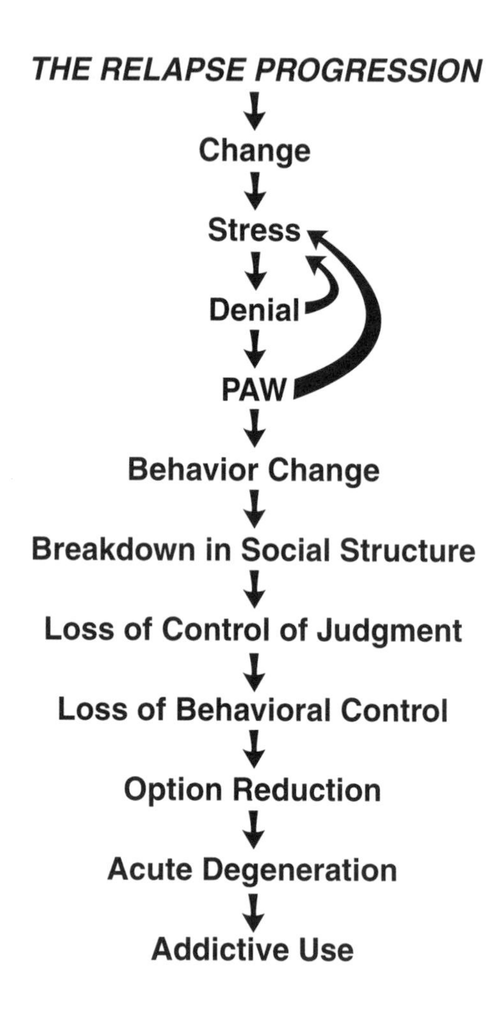
THE RELAPSE PROGRESSION
Change
Stress
Denial
PAW
Behavior Change
Breakdown in Social Structure
Loss of Control of Judgment
Loss of Behavioral Control
Option Reduction
Acute Degeneration
Addictive Use

process begins long before the person begins using. Remember that it begins silently within you. For a long period of time you will not be aware of the progression because it is taking place subconsciously.

There will be external warning signs, but you will not acknowledge them even to yourself unless you have learned to recognize the predictable pattern. People around you will probably not recognize them either because the relapse symptoms often look like the symptoms of other disorders.

The relapse syndrome is reversible with appropriate treatment. By learning to recognize the stages in the relapse process it is possible to interrupt the progression.

INTERRUPTING THE RELAPSE SYNDROME

Managing the symptoms of post acute withdrawal is the best method of relapse prevention. However, when you are already in an episode of dysfunction, it may be too late to utilize those methods, and you will need some help to become stabilized and to prevent further progression.

The first thing to do is to utilize an adequately controlled environment where you can be protected from the immediate crisis and from the availability of alcohol and drugs. If the episode is mild, some time in a quiet, calm environment will probably be sufficient for you to begin to reverse the process. If the situation is moderately severe it may be necessary to take some time off work and to plan some time away from places and people that intensify the problem.

If the relapse symptoms are severe, hospitalization may be necessary **before** using occurs or before you have a severe breakdown of another type. Sometimes persons in an acute dysfunction episode believe that if they do not use they will go crazy or kill themselves. You need to recognize in advance that there are other options available. Inpatient treatment is one of those options. It is better to choose to go to an inpatient program to prevent severe consequences than to go for detoxification.

There are people who would rather die than drink. That is why the rate of suicide is high among recovering alcoholics. This is very sad because it is possible to recover from alcohol or drug use, but it is not possible to recover from death. If you ever feel that your life is at risk because your pain is so severe that suicide is an option, seek IMMEDIATE help. There are other options that are not apparent to you through your pain.

It is important for you to recognize and to remember that there is no point at which you cannot interrupt the relapse syndrome if you know how to recognize it, if you know that there are constructive rather than destructive options, and if you recognize that you have a choice.

THE PHASES AND WARNING SIGNS OF RELAPSE

(Symptoms of External Dysfunction)

The relapse process causes the recovering person to feel pain and discomfort when not drinking. This pain and discomfort can become so severe that the recovering person becomes unable to live normally when not drinking, and feels that taking a drink cannot be any worse than the pain of staying sober. Thirty-seven warning signs of relapse were identified in 1973 by Terence Gorski through the completion of clinical interviews with 118 recovering patients. The recovering persons had four things in common: (1) they had completed a 21- or 28-day rehabilitation program for alcoholism; (2) they had recognized that they were recovering persons and could not safely use alcohol or drugs; (3) they had been discharged with the conscious intention of remaining permanently sober by using both Alcoholics Anonymous (AA) and professional outpatient counseling; and (4) they had eventually returned to drinking in spite of their initial comments to remain sober.

The most commonly reported symptoms in this clinical research were compiled in a Relapse Chart depicting the warning signs of a relapse. These symptoms have been divided into 10 phases and the wording has been changed slightly in order to be more easily understood.

Phase I: Internal Change: During this phase I look good on the outside, but I start using old addictive ways of thinking and managing feelings that make me feel bad on the inside. The most common relapse warning signs are:

☐ 1-1. ***Increased Stress:*** I begin to feel more stressed than usual. Sometimes this is the result of a problem or situation that is easy to see. At other times it is the result of little problems that cause stress to build up slowly over time.

☐ 1-2. ***Change in Thinking:*** I begin to think my recovery program is not as important as it used to be. Sometimes things are going so well that I don't believe I need to put a lot of effort into my program. At other times I have problems that my recovery program doesn't seem to help and I ask myself, "why bother?"

☐ 1-3. ***Change in Feeling:*** I start having unpleasant feelings that I don't like. Sometimes I feel euphoric, like everything is going my way when I know that it really is not. At other times I feel depressed, like nothing is working out. I know that these mood sweeps are not good for me.

☐ 1-4. ***Change in Behavior:*** I start acting different. I still look and sound good on the outside, but I know deep inside that I am not practicing my program the way I used to. Deep inside I know something is going wrong.

Phase II: Denial: During this phase, I stop paying attention to or honestly telling others what I am thinking

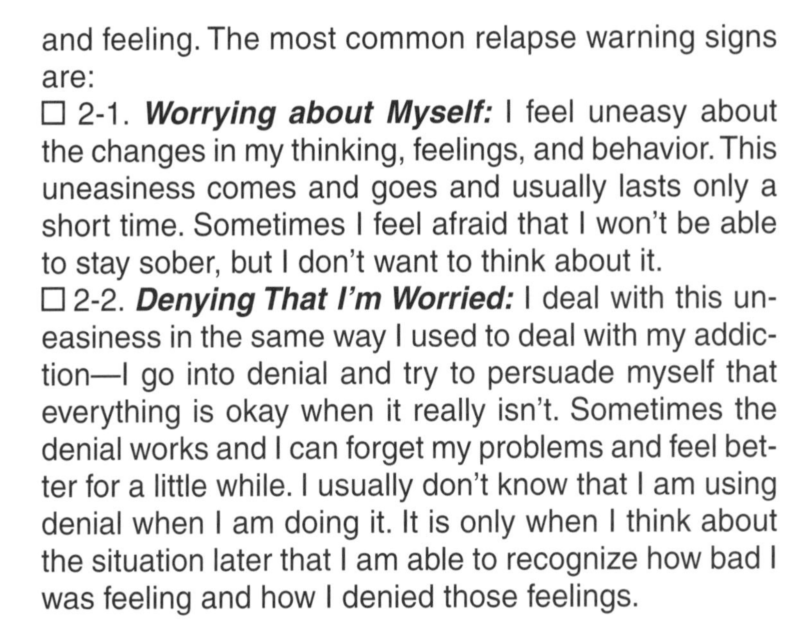

and feeling. The most common relapse warning signs are:

☐ 2-1. ***Worrying about Myself:*** I feel uneasy about the changes in my thinking, feelings, and behavior. This uneasiness comes and goes and usually lasts only a short time. Sometimes I feel afraid that I won't be able to stay sober, but I don't want to think about it.

☐ 2-2. ***Denying That I'm Worried:*** I deal with this uneasiness in the same way I used to deal with my addiction—I go into denial and try to persuade myself that everything is okay when it really isn't. Sometimes the denial works and I can forget my problems and feel better for a little while. I usually don't know that I am using denial when I am doing it. It is only when I think about the situation later that I am able to recognize how bad I was feeling and how I denied those feelings.

PHASE III: Avoidance and Defensiveness: During this phase, I try to avoid anyone or anything that will force me to be honest about how my thinking, feelings, and behavior have changed. If I am confronted directly, I get defensive and can't hear what others are trying to tell me. The most common relapse warning signs are:

☐ 3-1. ***Believing I'll Never Use Alcohol or Drugs:*** I convince myself that I don't need to put a lot of energy into my recovery program today because I will probably never go back to alcohol or drug use. I tend to keep this belief to myself. Sometimes I am afraid to tell my counselor or other recovering people about this belief for fear of being confronted. At other times I think that it is none of their business.

☐ 3-2. ***Worrying about Others Instead of Self:*** I take the focus off myself by becoming more concerned about the sobriety of others than about my personal recovery. I privately judge the drinking or using of my friends and spouse and the recovery programs of other recovering people. I keep these private judgments to myself and don't talk about them. This is often called "working the other guy's program."

☐ 3-3. ***Defensiveness:*** I feel reluctant to discuss personal problems and what I am doing in my recovery because I am afraid I will be criticized or confronted. I feel scared, angry, and defensive when other people ask me questions about my recovery program or point out things about my recovery that I don't want to see. I tend to get defensive even when no defense is necessary.

☐ 3-4. ***Compulsive Behavior:*** I start using compulsive behaviors to keep my mind off how uncomfortable I am feeling. I get stuck in old, rigid, and self-defeating ways of thinking and acting. I tend to do the same things over and over again without a good reason. I try to control conversations either by talking too much or not talking at all. I start working more than I need to and get involved in many activities. Other people think I am the model of recovery because of my heavy involvement in Twelve-Step work and chairing meetings. I become active in my therapy group by "playing therapist" but I am reluctant to talk about my personal problems. I avoid casual or informal involvement with people unless I can be in control.

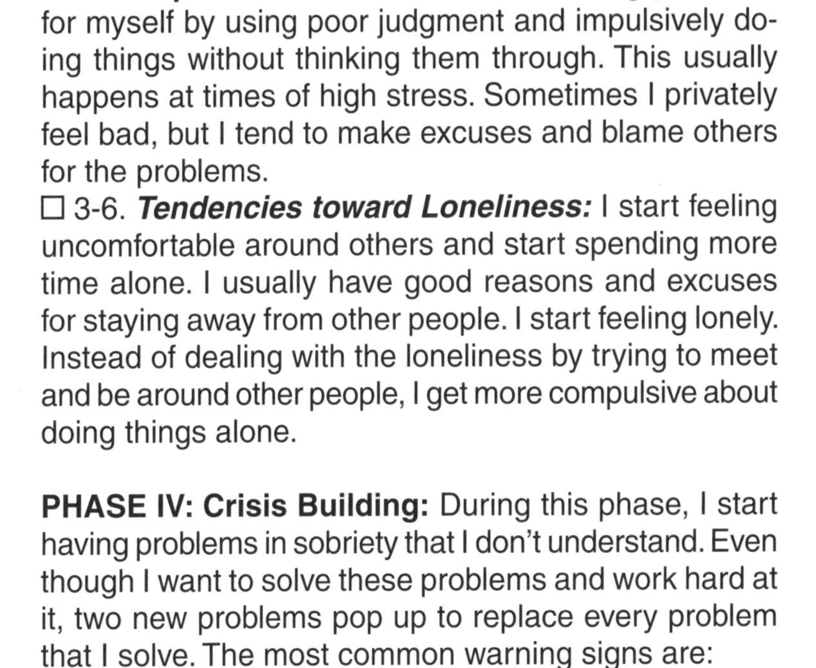

☐ 3-5. ***Impulsive Behavior:*** I start creating problems for myself by using poor judgment and impulsively doing things without thinking them through. This usually happens at times of high stress. Sometimes I privately feel bad, but I tend to make excuses and blame others for the problems.

☐ 3-6. ***Tendencies toward Loneliness:*** I start feeling uncomfortable around others and start spending more time alone. I usually have good reasons and excuses for staying away from other people. I start feeling lonely. Instead of dealing with the loneliness by trying to meet and be around other people, I get more compulsive about doing things alone.

PHASE IV: Crisis Building: During this phase, I start having problems in sobriety that I don't understand. Even though I want to solve these problems and work hard at it, two new problems pop up to replace every problem that I solve. The most common warning signs are:

☐ 4-1. ***Tunnel Vision:*** I start to think my life is made up of separate and unrelated parts. I focus on one small part of my life and block out everything else. Sometimes I focus only on the good things and block out or ignore the bad. In this way I can mistakenly believe everything is fine when it really isn't. At other times I see only what is going wrong and blow that out of proportion. This causes me to feel like nothing is going my way even when there are many good things happening in my life. As a result I can't see "the big picture" or figure out how what I do in one part of my life can cause problems in other parts of my life. When problems develop I don't know why. I believe that life is unfair and that I have no power to do anything about it.

☐ 4-2. ***Minor Depression:*** I start to feel depressed, down, blue, listless, and empty of feelings. I lack energy, tend to sleep too much, and rarely feel good or full of life. I am able to distract myself from these moods by getting busy with other things and not talking about the depression.

☐ 4-3. ***Loss of Constructive Planning:*** I stop planning ahead and thinking about what I am going to do next. I begin to think that the slogan, "One Day at a Time," means that I should not plan ahead or think about what I am going to do. I pay less and less attention to details. I become listless. My plans are based more on wishful thinking (how I wish things would be) than reality (how things actually are). As a result I make plans that are not realistic and stop paying attention to the details of implementing those plans.

☐ 4-4. ***Plans Begin to Fail:*** My plans begin to fail and each failure causes new problems. I tend to overreact to or mismanage each problem in a way that creates a new and bigger problem. I start having the same kind of problems with work, friends, family, and money that I used to have when I was using addictively. I feel guilty and remorseful

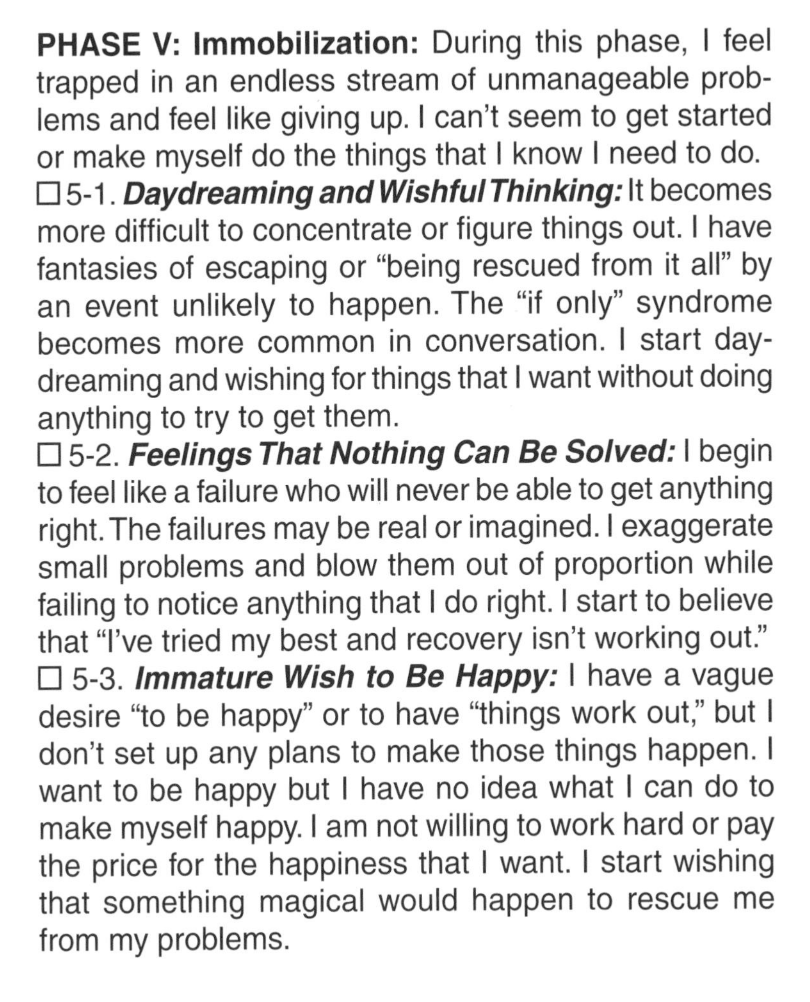

when I have these problems. I work hard trying to solve them, but something always seems to go wrong that creates an even bigger or more depressing problem.

PHASE V: Immobilization: During this phase, I feel trapped in an endless stream of unmanageable problems and feel like giving up. I can't seem to get started or make myself do the things that I know I need to do.

□ 5-1. ***Daydreaming and Wishful Thinking:*** It becomes more difficult to concentrate or figure things out. I have fantasies of escaping or "being rescued from it all" by an event unlikely to happen. The "if only" syndrome becomes more common in conversation. I start daydreaming and wishing for things that I want without doing anything to try to get them.

□ 5-2. ***Feelings That Nothing Can Be Solved:*** I begin to feel like a failure who will never be able to get anything right. The failures may be real or imagined. I exaggerate small problems and blow them out of proportion while failing to notice anything that I do right. I start to believe that "I've tried my best and recovery isn't working out."

□ 5-3. ***Immature Wish to Be Happy:*** I have a vague desire "to be happy" or to have "things work out," but I don't set up any plans to make those things happen. I want to be happy but I have no idea what I can do to make myself happy. I am not willing to work hard or pay the price for the happiness that I want. I start wishing that something magical would happen to rescue me from my problems.

PHASE VI: Confusion and Overreaction: During this phase I have trouble thinking clearly and managing my thoughts, feelings, and actions. I am irritable and tend to overreact to small things. The most common relapse warning signs are:

☐ 6-1. ***Difficulty in Thinking Clearly:*** I start to have trouble thinking clearly and solving usually simple problems. Sometimes my mind races and I can't shut it off while at other time it seems to shut off or go blank. My mind tends to wander and I have difficulty thinking about something for more than a few minutes. I get confused and have trouble figuring out how one thing relates to or affects other things. I also have difficulty deciding what to do next in order to manage my life and recovery. As a result I tend to make bad decisions that I would not have made if I were thinking clearly.

☐ 6-2. ***Difficulty in Managing Feelings and Emotions:*** I start to have difficulty managing my feelings and emotions. Sometimes I overreact emotionally and feel too much. At other times I become emotionally numb and can't figure out what I am feeling. Sometimes I feel strange or have "crazy feelings" for no apparent reason. I start to think that I might be going crazy. I have strong mood swings and periodically feel depressed, anxious, and scared. As a result, I don't trust my feelings and emotions and often try to ignore stuff, or forget about them. My mood sweeps start causing me new problems.

☐ 6-3. ***Difficulty in Remembering Things:*** At times I have problems remembering things and learning new information and skills. Things I want to remember seem to dissolve or evaporate from my mind within minutes. I also have problems remembering key events from my childhood, adolescence, or adulthood. At times I remember things clearly, but at other times these same memories will not come to mind. I feel blocked, stuck, or cut off from these memories. At times, the inability to remember things causes me to make bad decisions that I would not have made if my memory were working properly.

☐ 6-4. ***Periods of Confusion:*** I start getting confused more often, and the confusion is more severe and lasts longer. I'm not sure what is right or wrong. I don't know what to do to solve my problems because everything I try seems to make them worse. I get angry at myself because I can't solve my problems and just keep making things worse.

☐ 6-5. ***Difficulty in Managing Stress:*** I start having trouble dealing with stress. Sometimes I feel numb and can't recognize the minor signs of daily stress. At other times I seem overwhelmed by severe stress for no real reason. When I feel stressed out I cannot relax no matter what I do. The things other people do to relax either don't work for me or they make the stress worse. It seems I get so tense that I am not in control. The stress starts to get so bad that I can't do the things I normally do. I get afraid that I will collapse physically or emotionally.

☐ 6-6. ***Irritation with Friends:*** My relationships with friends, family, counselors, and other recovering people become strained. Sometimes I feel threatened when

others talk about the changes they are noticing in my behavior and moods. At other times I just don't care about what they say. The arguments and conflicts get worse despite my efforts to resolve them. I start to feel guilty.
☐ 6-7. ***Easily Angered:*** I feel irritable and frustrated. I start losing my temper for no real reason and feeling guilty afterward. I often overreact to small things that really shouldn't make any difference. I start avoiding people because I am afraid I might lose control and get violent. The effort to control myself adds to the stress and tension.

PHASE VII: Depression: During this phase I become so depressed that I can't do the things I normally do. At times I feel life is not worth living, and sometimes I think about killing myself or using alcohol or other drugs as a way to end the depression. I am so depressed that I can't hide it from others. The most common relapse warning signs are:
☐ 7-1. ***Irregular Eating Habits:*** I either start to overeat or I lose my appetite and eat very little. As a result I start gaining or losing weight. I skip meals and stop eating at regular times. I replace a well-balanced, nourishing diet with "junk food."
☐ 7-2. ***Lack of Desire to Take Action:*** I can't get started or get anything done. At those times I am unable to concentrate, feel anxious, fearful, uneasy, and often feel trapped with no way out.
☐ 7-3. ***Difficulty Sleeping Restfully:*** I cannot fall asleep.

When I do sleep, I have unusual or disturbing dreams, awaken many times, and have difficulty falling back to sleep. I sleep fitfully and rarely experience a deep, relaxing sleep. I awaken from a night of sleep feeling tired. The times of day during which I sleep change. At times I stay up late due to an inability to fall asleep and then oversleep because I am too tired to get up in the morning. At other times I become so exhausted that I sleep for extremely long periods, sometimes sleeping around the clock for one or more days.

☐ 7-4. ***Loss of Daily Structure:*** My daily routine becomes haphazard. I stop getting up and going to bed at regular times. I start skipping meals and eating at unusual times. I find it hard to keep appointments and plan social events. I feel rushed and overburdened at times and then have nothing to do at other times. I am unable to follow through on plans and decisions and experience tension, frustration, fear, or anxiety which keeps me from doing what I know needs to be done.

☐ 7-5. ***Periods of Deep Depression:*** I feel depressed more often. The depression becomes worse, lasts longer, and interferes with living. The depression is so bad it is noticed by others and cannot be easily denied. The depression is most severe during unplanned or unstructured periods of time. Fatigue, hunger, and loneliness make the depression worse. When I feel depressed I separate from other people, become irritable and angry with others, and often complain that nobody cares or understands what I am going through.

PHASE VIII: Behavioral Loss of Control: During this phase I can't control my thoughts, feelings, and behavior. I can't stick to a productive daily schedule. I am still denying how dysfunctional I have become, and I am not willing to admit that I am out of control even though my life is chaotic and I have serious problems. The most common warning signs are:

☐ 8-1. ***Irregular Attendance at AA and Treatment Meetings:*** I start finding excuses to miss therapy and self-help group meetings. I find excuses to justify this and don't recognize the importance of AA and treatment. I develop the attitude that "AA and counseling aren't making me feel better, so why should I make them a number-one priority? Other things are more important."

☐ 8-2. ***An "I Don't Care" Attitude:*** I try to act as if I don't care about the problems that are occurring. This is to hide feelings of helplessness and a growing lack of self-respect and self-confidence.

☐ 8-3. ***Open Rejection of Help:*** I cut myself off from people who can help. I may do this by having fits of anger that drive others away, by criticizing and putting others down, or by quietly withdrawing from others.

☐ 8-4. ***Dissatisfaction with Life:*** Things seem so bad that I begin to think I might as well go back to alcohol or drug use because things couldn't get worse. Life seems to have become unmanageable even though I am sober and not using addictively.

☐ 8-5. ***Feelings of Powerlessness and Helplessness:***

I have trouble "getting started." I have difficulty thinking clearly, concentrating, and thinking abstractly. I feel that I can't do anything and begin to believe there is no way out.

PHASE IX: Recognition of Loss of Control: During this phase my denial breaks and I suddenly recognize how severe my problems are, how unmanageable life has become, and how little power and control I have to solve any of the problems. This awareness is very painful and frightening. By this time I have become so isolated that it seems that there is no one to turn to for help. The most common warning signs are:

☐ 9-1. ***Difficulty with Physical Coordination and Accidents:*** I start having difficulty with physical coordination that results in dizziness, poor balance, difficulty with hand-eye coordination, or slow reflexes. These problems cause me to feel clumsy and become accident prone.

☐ 9-2. ***Self-pity:*** I begin to feel sorry for myself and may use self-pity to get attention at AA or from family members. I feel ashamed because I think I must be crazy, emotionally disturbed, defective as a person, or incapable of being or feeling normal. I also feel guilty because I believe I am doing things wrong or failing to work a proper recovery program. The shame and guilt cause me to hide the warning signs and stop talking honestly with others about what I am experiencing. The longer I keep the warning signs hidden, the stronger they become. I try to manage the warning signs and find that

I can't do it. As a result I begin to believe that I must be hopeless and I feel sorry for myself.

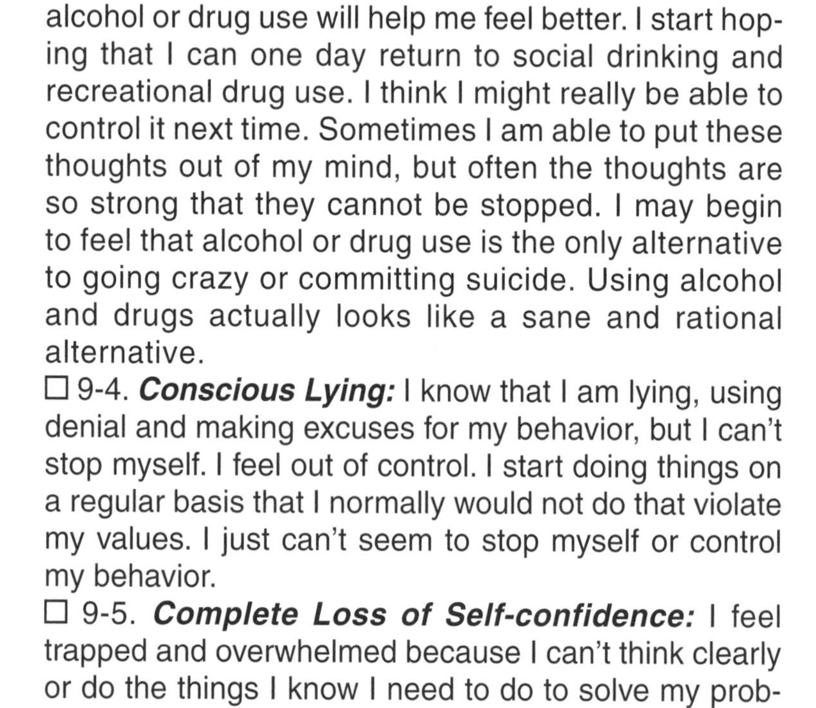

☐ 9-3. ***Thoughts of Social Use:*** I start to think that alcohol or drug use will help me feel better. I start hoping that I can one day return to social drinking and recreational drug use. I think I might really be able to control it next time. Sometimes I am able to put these thoughts out of my mind, but often the thoughts are so strong that they cannot be stopped. I may begin to feel that alcohol or drug use is the only alternative to going crazy or committing suicide. Using alcohol and drugs actually looks like a sane and rational alternative.

☐ 9-4. ***Conscious Lying:*** I know that I am lying, using denial and making excuses for my behavior, but I can't stop myself. I feel out of control. I start doing things on a regular basis that I normally would not do that violate my values. I just can't seem to stop myself or control my behavior.

☐ 9-5. ***Complete Loss of Self-confidence:*** I feel trapped and overwhelmed because I can't think clearly or do the things I know I need to do to solve my problems. I feel powerless and hopeless. I start to believe that I am useless, incompetent, and will never be able to manage my life.

Phase X: Option Reduction: During this phase I feel trapped by the pain and inability to manage my life. I start to believe that there are only three ways out—insanity, suicide, or self-medication with alcohol or drugs. I no longer believe anyone or anything can help me. The most common warning signs that occur during this phase are:

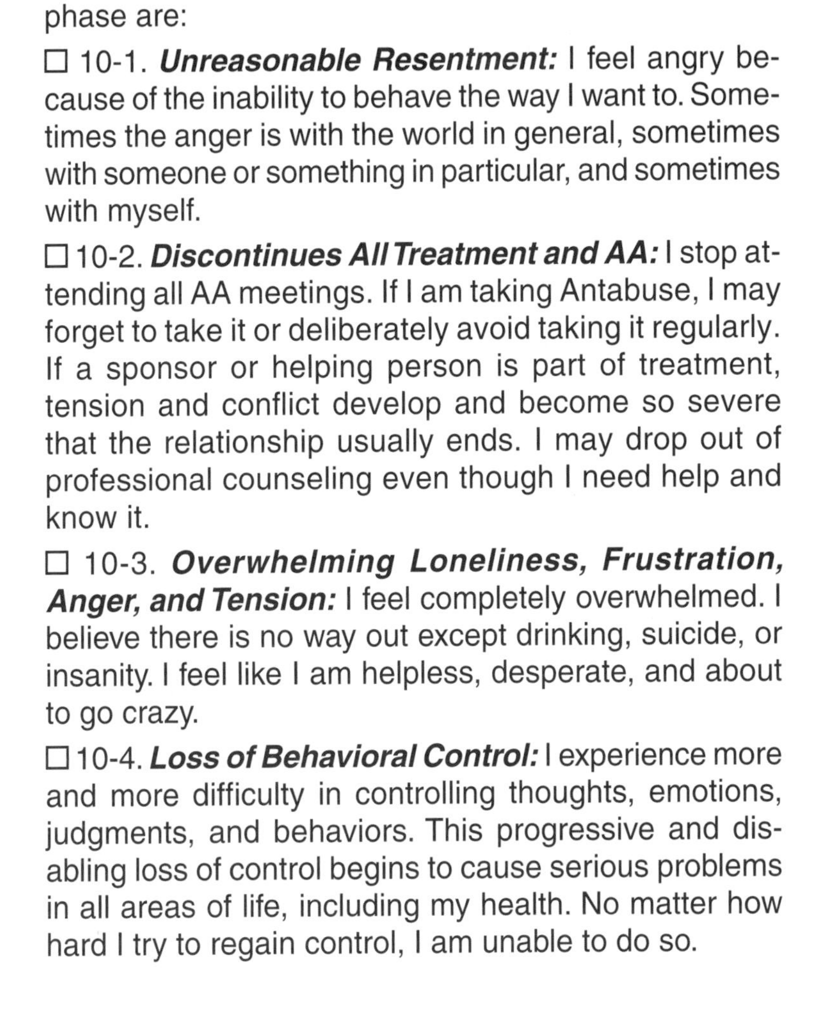

☐ 10-1. ***Unreasonable Resentment:*** I feel angry because of the inability to behave the way I want to. Sometimes the anger is with the world in general, sometimes with someone or something in particular, and sometimes with myself.

☐ 10-2. ***Discontinues All Treatment and AA:*** I stop attending all AA meetings. If I am taking Antabuse, I may forget to take it or deliberately avoid taking it regularly. If a sponsor or helping person is part of treatment, tension and conflict develop and become so severe that the relationship usually ends. I may drop out of professional counseling even though I need help and know it.

☐ 10-3. ***Overwhelming Loneliness, Frustration, Anger, and Tension:*** I feel completely overwhelmed. I believe there is no way out except drinking, suicide, or insanity. I feel like I am helpless, desperate, and about to go crazy.

☐ 10-4. ***Loss of Behavioral Control:*** I experience more and more difficulty in controlling thoughts, emotions, judgments, and behaviors. This progressive and disabling loss of control begins to cause serious problems in all areas of life, including my health. No matter how hard I try to regain control, I am unable to do so.

PHASE XI: Alcohol and Drug Use: During this phase I return to alcohol or drug use, try to control it, lose control, and realize that my addiction is once again destroying my life.

☐ 11-1. ***Attempting Controlled Use:*** I convince myself that I have no choice but to use alcohol or drugs and that using will somehow make my problems better or allow me to escape from them for a little while. I plan to try either social use or a short-term binge. If I try to be a controlled social or recreational user, I start using a little bit on a regular basis. If I decide to go out on a short-term binge, I plan a chemical-use episode that will be a "one-time only, time-limited, controlled binge."

☐ 11-2. ***Disappointment, Shame, and Guilt:*** I feel disappointed because alcohol and drugs don't do for me what I thought they would. I feel guilty because I believe I have done something wrong by using addictively. I feel ashamed because I start to believe I am defective and worthless as a person, and my relapse proves it.

☐ 11-3. ***Loss of Control:*** My alcohol or drug use spirals out of control. Sometimes I lose control slowly. At other times, the loss of control is very rapid. I begin using as often and as much as before.

☐ 11-4. ***Life and Health Problems:*** I start having severe problems with my life and health. Marriage, jobs, and friendships are seriously damaged. Eventually, my physical health suffers and I become so ill that I need professional treatment.

THE RELAPSE SYNDROME

Internal Dysfunction

- ***Thought Impairment***
- ***Emotional Impairment***
- ***Memory Problems***
- ***High Stress***
- ***Sleep Problems***
- ***Coordination Problems***

External Dysfunction

- ***Denial Returns***
- ***Avoidance and Defensiveness***
- ***Crisis Building***
- ***Immobilization***
- ***Confusion and Overreaction***

Loss of Control

- ***Depression***
- ***Loss of Behavioral Control***
- ***Recognition of Loss of Control***
- ***Option Reduction***
- ***Relapse Episode***

Chapter VIII

RELAPSE PREVENTION PLANNING

Most relapse in addiction is unnecessary. Many alcoholics relapse because they do not understand the process and what to do to prevent it. Appropriate action on your part and the people in your life can prevent or interrupt the relapse syndrome before the consequences become tragic. Planning for relapse minimizes its destructive potential. Relapse prevention planning can give you a sense of security. You will know that you are doing what is necessary to avoid relapse. You can identify early warning signs and develop a plan for interrupting the relapse syndrome if it appears. Relapse prevention planning should be an essential part of your recovery program. (195) (203)

Prevention planning for relapse minimizes its destructive potential.

The steps of relapse prevention planning are:

1. ***Stabilization:*** Get control of yourself.

2. ***Self-Assessment:*** Find out what is going on in your head, heart, and life.

3. ***Relapse Education:*** Learn about relapse and what to do to prevent it.

4. ***Warning Sign Identification:*** Make a list of your personal relapse warning signs.

5. ***Warning Sign Management:*** Learn how to interrupt warning signs before you lose control.

6. ***Inventory Training:*** Learn how to become consciously aware of warning signs as they develop.

7. ***Review the Recovery Program:*** Make sure your recovery program is able to help you to manage your warning signs.

8. ***Involvement of Significant Others:*** Teach others how to work with you to avoid relapse.

9. ***Follow-Up:*** Up-date your relapse prevention plan regularly.

---

1. STABILIZATION—I must get back in control of myself and my behavior.

---

1. ***Stabilization:*** Before you can do relapse prevention planning you must be in control of yourself. Stabilization means the process of regaining control of your thoughts, emotions, memory, judgment, and behavior, after you have relapsed. This is a time of crisis for you and your family. The relapse has disrupted your life. It is normal for all of you to feel frightened, angry, disappointed, and guilty. You need help. You need to turn to people you can trust and depend on and who can help you take the steps necessary to reestablish your sobriety. If you are unable to maintain consistent control of your thoughts, emotions, and behavior you should consult a professional counselor or treatment center. You may need professional help in getting stabilized.

---

2. ASSESSMENT—I must figure out, with the help of others, what is causing the relapse episodes.

---

2. ***Assessment:*** The second step of relapse prevention planning is to discover what happened that caused the relapse. This is done by reviewing your history of addictive using as well as specific warning signs and symptoms that occurred during each period of attempted

abstinence. This information will provide valuable clues as to what went wrong and what can be done differently to improve your chances at permanent sobriety. Remember that your past is your best teacher. If you fail to

3. *EDUCATION—I must learn about the process of relapse and how to prevent it.*

learn from your past you are condemned to repeat it. 3. ***Education:*** In order to prevent relapse you must understand it. The more information you have about addiction, recovery, and relapse the more tools you have in your possession to maintain your recovery. You need to understand post acute withdrawal symptoms, what puts you in high risk of developing them, what might trigger them, and what it takes to prevent or manage them. You should be very familiar with the warning signs and be able to give examples of them and to put them into your own words to be sure you understand them. You have already begun the education process by reading this book. But reading alone is insufficient. The concepts presented in this book must be reviewed and discussed with other people. A certified addictions counselor should be involved in helping you review this material. If that is not possible your AA sponsor or another adult who has read the book and does not have an active drinking or addictions problem can help you review and apply this information. Remember, the education program is not completed until you are capable of honestly and openly applying the information you have learned to your own life and your current life circumstances. Addiction is a disease of denial. Without involving others in the education process, your denial may prevent you from recognizing what is really happening to you.

4. WARNING SIGN IDENTIFICATION—I must identify the warning signs that tell me I'm in trouble with my sobriety.

4. ***Relapse Warning Sign Identification:*** Every person has a unique set of personal warning signs that indicate that the process of relapse is occurring. These are signals that you give to yourself and to others that you are in danger of alcohol or drug use or of developing some other relapse symptoms. Relapse warning sign identification is the process of identifying the problems and symptoms that can lead you to relapse. Problems may be situations outside of yourself or within. Symptoms may be health problems, thinking problems, emotional

problems, memory problems, or problems with judgment and appropriate behavior.

It is necessary to develop a list of ***personal*** warning signs or indications that you may be in danger. The warning list should be developed from past relapse experiences. From the list of warning signs, select about five that you believe apply to you. Put these into your

---

5. WARNING SIGN MANAGEMENT—I must have concrete plans for preventing and stopping warning signs.

---

own words and write a statement about each one that describes your own experience with this warning sign. You should develop a list of clear and specific indicators that you are moving away from productive and comfortable living and beginning to move toward relapse.

5. ***Warning Sign Management:*** Each warning sign is actually a problem that you need to prevent or solve once it occurs. If you want to avoid problems, you will need to review each warning sign and answer the question: "How can I prevent this problem from happening?"

You must remember that addiction is a disease with a tendency toward relapse. This means that any recovering addict will have a tendency to experience problems or warning signs that can lead them back to addictive use. Once you know and accept that fact, you can plan for the inevitable. You will have problems and relapse warning signs. If you want to avoid relapse, you will need to take each warning sign that you have experienced in the past and develop a plan for coping with it should it develop.

It is essential for you to establish new responses to the identified warning signs of relapse. Determine what you are going to do when you recognize that a specific warning sign is working in your life. How can the relapse syndrome be interrupted? What positive action can you take that will remove the relapse warning sign? List several options or possible solutions for removing the problem from your life.

Listing several alternatives will give more chance of choosing the best solution and give you alternatives if the first choice does not work. Choose a reasonable option that seems to offer the best possibility of interrupting the relapse process. This will be your new response when you become aware of a particular warning sign.

Practice each new response until it becomes a habit. If the new response is to be available to you in times of high stress, you must practice it in times of low stress. Practice and practice until the response becomes a habit. If the new response fails to interrupt the warning sign, establish a new and more effective plan.

You cannot afford to put off developing a plan to interrupt your warning signs if they occur. If you do not have a plan, you will not be able to interrupt them when they occur.

---

6. INVENTORY TRAINING—I must do an inventory twice daily so I can notice the first signs of trouble and correct the problems before they get out of control.

---

6. ***Inventory Training:*** Any successful recovery program involves daily inventory. AA Step 10 reminds us that we should continue to take personal inventory, and when we are wrong promptly admit it. A daily inventory is necessary to help you identify relapse warning signs before your denial is reactivated. Any relapse warning sign is serious because it can be the first step toward taking a drink or physical or emotional collapse. Without a daily inventory, you will probably ignore early warning signs, and then be unable to interrupt the relapse syndrome when it becomes more apparent.

For a relapse prevention plan you should design a special inventory system that monitors the warning signs of potential relapse. Develop a way to incorporate this inventory system into your day-to-day living. You now have a list of your personal warning signs. How are you going to determine if any of those symptoms have been activated in your life?

In order for a daily inventory to become a habit, we recommend that you establish two daily inventory rituals. The first should occur in the morning. Clear five to ten minutes to read the daily entry in the Twenty-Four-Hour-A-Day Book and to briefly outline your plans for the day. Ask yourself if you are prepared for this day and what you can do that will help you physically and emotionally to meet the challenges of the day and to maintain a comfortable sobriety.

The second inventory ritual should occur in the evening. Review the tasks of the day, identify what you handled well and what needs improving. What strengths did you use in meeting the challenges of the day? How can you reinforce and build upon your strength? What weaknesses became apparent and how can you correct those shortcomings, and improve in those areas?

Look carefully at your list of personal relapse warning signs. Are any of these present in your life? If so, what are you doing to correct those situations? Are there other warning signs that you see that should be added to your list?

It may be helpful for you to keep a daily journal to review your recovery progress and to help you monitor for relapse warning signs. This will help you see that you are making progress in your recovery. It is, after all, progress that we strive for, not perfection. Just knowing what your warning signs are is not necessarily going to help you. Remember the warning signs of relapse often develop unconsciously. You do not know that they are happening to you. An inventory is a way to consciously review what happens to you on a daily basis. Through a twice daily inventory, morning and evening, it is possible to become aware of relapse warning signs early, and do something to stop them before you lose control.

> ***7. REVIEW OF THE RECOVERY PROGRAM—I must review my current recovery program to be sure there is help in coping with my warning signs.***

---

7. ***Review of the Recovery Program:*** Recovery and relapse are opposite sides of the same coin. If you are not in the process of recovering, you are in danger of relapsing. A good recovery program is necessary to prevent relapse. Has your previous recovery program been working for you? How can it be improved? You must learn to challenge yourself in your day-to-day living. Are you acknowledging your addiction and managing its symptoms? Are you attending to your overall health needs? Are you doing everything necessary to recover? Develop a new recovery program based on what has

worked for you and what has not worked for you in the past. For every problem, symptom, or warning sign you identified you need to be sure there is something in your recovery program to help you cope with it.

> ***8. INVOLVEMENT OF OTHERS—I must ask others to help me stay sober by telling them about my warning signs and asking for feedback if they see any warning signs develop.***

---

8. ***Involvement of Significant Others:*** You cannot recover in isolation. Total recovery involves the help and support of a variety of persons. You need others for a successful relapse prevention plan. The relapse process is often a totally unconscious process. Despite daily inventory you may not be able to see what is happening. That is why it is important to involve other people in your relapse prevention plans. Family members, co-workers, and fellow AA members can be extremely helpful in helping to recognize warning signs while it is still possible to do something about them.

In order for others to help you, they must know about your relapse warning signs and care about you enough to be willing to tell you when they notice these warning signs. You must be willing to talk with these people on a regular basis so they will notice when something is going wrong. You must also be willing to listen and act upon what they say.

Select significant individuals in your life to become involved in relapse prevention. They can be your immediate family members, a supportive employer, close friends, an AA sponsor, or AA friends.

Make a list of all the people with whom you have daily contact. Select from that list those people that you think would be important in helping you stay sober and avoid relapse. These people will form your intervention network. Determine how each person has interacted with you in the past when you have shown symptoms of relapse. Has it been helpful to your sobriety? What could they have done that would have been more helpful to your recovery? Now determine what you would like each of these people to do the next time symptoms of relapse are recognized.

Bring these people in your life together for a meeting. Explain to them your list of personal warning signs and form a contract with each support person as to what he or she will do when relapse symptoms are recognized and what they will do if you begin using. What do you want them to do and what are they willing to do if your denial is reactivated and you become unable to recognize that there is a problem?

You and your intervention network should rehearse or role play a situation when you might be at your worst.

Role play a situation in which you are showing warning signs and then deny these symptoms. Allow them to rehearse what they will do to help you interrupt your relapse syndrome.

Allow the intervention network to participate in your recovery. Encourage them to support your recovery program and to refuse to support your relapse warning symptoms. Remember, too, that the members of your family are also recovering. You must acknowledge their needs and make a strong commitment to assist them in their own recovery programs.

---

9. FOLLOW-UP AND REINFORCEMENT—I must revise my relapse prevention plan at regular intervals as I grow and change in recovery.

---

9. ***Follow-Up and Reinforcement:*** Addiction does not go away. It is lifelong chronic disease. Recovery from addiction is a way of life. Since relapse prevention planning is part of recovery, it too must become a way of life.

Relapse prevention planning must be integrated into your entire life and every aspect of your recovery. Your relapse prevention plan must be compatible with AA and other support groups you are using to maintain ongoing sobriety. It should also be compatible with your treatment program and that of your family.

Relapse prevention must be practiced until it becomes a habit. We are all enslaved by our habits. The only freedom we can find is to choose carefully the habits to which we allow ourselves to become enslaved. For the recovering person, it is especially true that there is freedom in structure. It is only in the habit and structure of a daily sobriety program that you can find freedom from enslavement to addiction.

You must be willing to revise and up-date your relapse prevention plans at regular intervals and be willing to recognize new problems that jeopardize your sobriety. Relapse prevention planning is a process that should become an integral part of your recovery. The outcome for you will be freedom to enjoy a comfortable sobriety and the assurance that you have an understanding of relapse, that you can identify your own warning signs, and that you have an action plan to interrupt those warning signs should they develop.

Chapter IX

FAMILY INVOLVEMENT IN THE RELAPSE SYNDROME

In many cases the addict is the first family member to seek treatment. Other family members become involved in order to help the alcoholic get sober. Many family members refuse to consider the fact that they have a problem that requires specialized treatment. These family members tend to deny their role in the addicted family and scapegoat personal and family problems upon the addicted person. They develop unrealistic expectations of how family life will improve with abstinence. When these expectations are not met, they blame the addict for the failure, even though he or she may be successfully following a recovery program. Their attitudes and behaviors can become such complicating factors in the addict's recovery that they can contribute to relapse.

Family members can be powerful allies in preventing relapse in the addict. (81) Relapse Prevention Planning utilizes the family's motivation to get the addict sober. As family members become involved in relapse prevention planning, a strong focus is placed upon coaddiction and its role in family relapse. Family members are helped to recognize their own coaddiction and become actively involved in their own treatment. Addiction is presented as a family disease that affects all family members, requiring them to get treatment. The addict needs treatment for addiction. Other family members need treatment for coaddiction.

The term "coaddiction" is sometimes used to refer only to the spouse of an addict and other terms are used to refer to other family members. We are using the term "coaddict" to refer to ANYONE WHOSE LIFE HAS BECOME UNMANAGEABLE AS A RESULT OF LIVING IN A COMMITTED RELATIONSHIP WITH AN ADDICTED PERSON.

Coaddiction is a definable syndrome that is chronic and follows a predictable progression. When persons in a committed relationship with an addicted person attempt to control drinking, drug use, or addictive behavior (over which they are powerless), they lose control over their own behavior (over which they can have power) and their lives become unmanageable.

When you try to control
What you are powerless over
You lose control
Over what you can manage.

The person suffering from coaddiction develops physical, psychological, and social symptoms as a result of attempting to adapt to and compensate for the debilitating effects of the stress of living with addiction.

As the coaddiction progresses, the stress-related symptoms become habitual. The symptoms also become self-reinforcing; that is, the presence of one symptom of coaddiction will automatically trigger other coaddiction symptoms. The coaddiction eventually becomes independent of the addiction that originally caused it. The symptoms of coaddiction will continue even if the alcoholic becomes sober or joins AA, or the coaddict ends the relationship.

The condition of coaddiction manifests itself in three stages of progression.

Early Stage: Normal Problem Solving and Attempts to Adjust

The normal reaction within any family to pain, to crisis, and to the dysfunction of one member of the family is to reduce the pain, ease the crisis, and to assist the dysfunctional member in order to protect the family. These responses do not make things better when the problem is addiction, because these measures deprive the addicted person of the painful learning experiences that bring an awareness that the addiction is creating problems. At this stage, coaddiction is simply a reaction to the symptoms of addictive disease. It is a normal response to an abnormal situation.

Middle Stage: Habitual Self-Defeating Responses

When the culturally prescribed responses to stress and crisis do not bring relief from the pain created by the addiction in the family, the family members TRY HARDER. They do the same things, only more often, more intensely, more desperately. They try to be more supportive, more helpful, more protective. They take on the responsibilities of the addicted person, not realizing that this causes the addict to become more irresponsible.

Things get worse instead of better and the sense of failure intensifies the response. Family members experience frustration, anxiety, and guilt. There is growing self-blame, lowering of self-concept, and self-defeating behaviors. They become isolated. They focus on addictive behavior and their attempt to control it. They have little time to focus on anything else. As a result they lose touch with the normal world outside of their family.

Chronic Stage: Family Collapse and Stress Degeneration

The continued, habitual response to addiction in the family results in specific repetitive, circular patterns of self-defeating behavior. These behavior patterns are independent and self-reinforcing and will persist even in the absence of the symptoms of addictive disease.

The things the family members have done in a sincere effort to help have failed. The resulting despair and guilt bring about confusion and chaos and the inability to interrupt dysfunctional behavior even when they are aware that what they are doing is not helping. The thinking and behavior of the coaddict is OUT OF CONTROL, and these thinking and behavior patterns will continue independent of the addiction.

Coaddict degeneration is bio-psycho-social. The ineffective attempts to control drinking and drinking behavior elevate chronic stress to the point of producing stress-related physical illnesses such as migraine headaches, ulcers, and hypertension. This chronic stress may also result in a nervous breakdown or other emotional illnesses. Out-of-control behavior itself is an addiction-centered lifestyle that pervades all life activity, even that which seems unrelated to the addiction. Social degeneration occurs as the addiction focus interferes with relationships and social activity. Spiritual degeneration results as the focus on the problem becomes so pervasive that there is no interest in anything beyond it, particularly concerns and needs related to a higher meaning of life.

Recovery from coaddiction means learning to accept and detach from the symptoms of addiction. It means learning to manage and control the symptoms of coaddiction. It means learning to focus on personal needs and personal growth, learning to respect and like oneself. It means learning to ***choose*** appropriate behavior. It means learning to be in control of one's own life.

Because it is a chronic condition, coaddiction, like addiction, is subject to relapse. But a condition of coaddict relapse may be more difficult to identify. Without an ongoing recovery program and proper care of oneself, old feelings and behaviors thought to be under control may surface and become out of control. Life again becomes unmanageable; ***the coaddict is in relapse.***

RELAPSE WARNING SIGNS FOR COADDICTION

From the observation of counselors who have worked with recovering family members, relapse warning signs for the coaddicted spouse have emerged. The following list has been compiled from these observations. (90)*

1. **Situational Loss of Daily Structure.** The family member's daily routine is interrupted by a temporary situation such as illness, the children's schedule, the holidays, vacation, etc. After the event or illness, the spouse does not return to all of the activities of his or her recovery program.

2. **Lack of Personal Care.** The spouse becomes careless about personal appearance and may stop doing and enjoying small things that are "just for own personal enjoyment." The person returns to taking care of others first and self second or third.

3. **Inability to Effectively Set and Maintain Limits.** The spouse begins to experience behavioral problems with the children. Limits that are being set tend to be too lenient or too rigid and result in more discipline problems.

*We want to thank Jan Smith for her help in compiling this list.

4. **Loss of Constructive Planning.** The spouse begins to feel confused and overwhelmed by personal responsibilities. Instead of deciding what is most important and doing that, he or she begins to react by doing the first thing that presents itself, while more important jobs go undone.

5. **Indecision.** The family member becomes more and more unable to make decisions related to daily life.

6. **Compulsive Behavior.** The spouse experiences episodes during which he or she feels driven to do more. Whatever has already been done does not seem to be enough.

7. **Fatigue or Lack of Rest.** He or she becomes unable to sleep the number of hours necessary to feel rested. When sleep does occur, it is fitful.

8. **Return of Unreasonable Resentments.** The spouse finds himself or herself mentally reviewing persons or events that have hurt, angered, or been generally upsetting. As these are reviewed, the spouse relives the old emotions and feels resentments about them.

9. **Return of the Tendency to Control People, Situations, and Things.** As the coaddicted person feels less control over life, he or she begins openly to try to control and manipulate other people or situations. The

addicted person may be the prime target, but does not necessarily have to be.

10. **Defensiveness.** The codependent person may not totally approve of some of his or her actions, but when challenged will openly justify the actions in a sharp or angry way.

11. **Self-Pity.** The coaddict begins to dwell on problems from the present or the past and in turn begins to magnify them. The person may ask, "Why does everything always happen to me?"

12. **Overspending/Worrying about Money.** The spouse may be very concerned about the family finances, yet impulsively spend money in order to "feel better." He or she becomes convinced that what was purchased was deserved, but feels guilty and even more trapped.

13. **Eating Disorder.** The family member "loses" his or her appetite to the point that even favorite foods are not appealing. Or the spouse may begin to overeat, regardless of appetite, in order to feel better. The overeating satisfies for only a very short time, or not at all.

14. **Scapegoating.** There is an increasing tendency to place the blame on other people, places, and things. The coaddict looks outside of self for the reasons why he or she is feeling bad.

15. **Return of Fear and General Anxiety.** The spouse begins to experience periods of time when he or she is nervous. Situations which previously did not cause fear or anxiety are now causing those emotions. The spouse may not even know the source of the nervousness.

16. **Loss of Belief in a Higher Power.** The spouse begins to lose belief in a higher power, whatever it may be. There is a tendency to rely more on self alone, or to turn to the addict for the strength and the solutions.

17. **Attendance at Al-Anon Becomes Sporadic.** The spouse changes the pattern of Al-Anon meeting attendance. He or she may go to fewer meetings, thinking there isn't time, the meetings aren't helping, or are not needed.

18. **Mind Racing.** The spouse feels as though he or she is on a treadmill that is going too fast. Despite attempts to slow down, the mind continues to race with the many things that are undone or the problems that are unsolved.

19. **Inability to Construct a Logical Chain of Thought.** The spouse tries to solve problems and gets stuck on something that would normally be simple. It seems that his or her mind does not work anymore, that it is impossible to figure out the world. As a result, he or she feels powerless and frustrated with life.

20. **Confusion.** The spouse knows that there are many feelings inside, but does not know what is actually wrong.

21. **Sleep Disturbance.** Sleeplessness or fitful nights become more regular. The more the person tries to sleep, the less he or she is able to. Sleep may come, but it is not restful. The spouse looks tired in the morning instead of rested.

22. **Artificial Emotion.** The coaddict begins to exhibit feelings without a conscious knowledge of why. He or she may become emotional for no reason at all.

23. **Behavioral Loss of Control.** The coaddict begins to lose control of his or her temper especially around the addict and/or the children. Loss of behavioral control is exhibited in such ways as overpunishing the children, hitting and yelling at the addict, or throwing things.

24. **Uncontrollable Mood Swings.** Changes in the coaddict's moods happen without any warning. The shifts are dramatic. He or she no longer feels somewhat down or somewhat happy, but instead goes from feeling extremely happy to extremely low.

25. **Failure to Maintain Interpersonal (informal) Support Systems.** The coaddict stops reaching out to friends and family. This may happen very gradually. He or

she turns down invitations for coffee, misses family gatherings, and no longer makes or returns phone calls.

26. **Feelings of Loneliness and Isolation.** The coaddict begins to spend more time alone. He or she usually rationalizes this behavior—too busy, the children, school, job, etc. Instead of dealing with the loneliness, the coaddict becomes more compulsive and impulsive. The isolation may be justified by convincing himself or herself that no one understands or really cares.

27. **Tunnel Vision.** No matter what the issue or situation might be, the coaddict focuses in on his or her opinion or decision and is unable to see other points of view. He or she is close-minded.

28. **Return of Periods of Free Floating Anxiety and/or Panic Attacks.** The coaddict may begin to reexperience, or experience for the first time, waves of anxiety that seem to occur for no specific reason. He or she may feel afraid and not know why. These uncontrollable feelings may snowball to the point that he or she is living in fear of fear.

29. **Health Problems.** Physical problems begin to occur such as headaches, migraines, stomach aches, chest pains, rashes, or allergies.

30. **Use of Medication or Alcohol as a Means to Cope.**

Desperate to gain some kind of relief from the physical and/or emotional pain, the coaddict may begin to drink, use drugs, or take prescription medications. The alcohol or drug use provides temporary relief from the growing problems.

31. **Total Abandonment of Support Meetings and Therapy Sessions.** Due to a variety of reasons (belief that he or she no longer needs the meetings, immobilizing fear, resentment, etc.), the coaddict completely stops going to support meetings or to therapy or both.

32. **Inability to Change Self-Defeating Behaviors.** While there is recognition by the coaddict that what is being done is not good for himself or herself, there is still the compulsion to continue the behavior despite that knowledge.

33. **Development of an "I Don't Care" Attitude.** It is easier to believe that "I don't care" than it is to believe that "I am out of control." In order to defend self-esteem, the coaddict rationalizes, "I don't care." As a result, a shift in value system occurs. Things that were once important now seem to be ignored.

34. **Complete Loss of Daily Structure.** The coaddict loses the belief that an orderly life is possible. He or she begins missing (forgetting) appointments or meetings, is unable to have scheduled meals, to go to bed or get up

on time. The coaddict is unable to perform simple acts of daily function.

35. **Despair and Suicidal Ideation.** The coaddict begins to believe that the situation is hopeless. He or she feels that options are reduced to two or three choices: going insane, committing suicide, or numbing out with medication, and/or alcohol.

36. **Major Physical Collapse.** The physical symptoms become so severe that medical attention is required. These can be any of a number of symptoms that become so severe that they render the coaddict dysfunctional (e.g., ulcers, migraines, heart pains, or heart palpitations).

37. **Major Emotional Collapse.** Having seemingly tried everything to cope, the coaddict can conceive no way to deal with his or her unmanageable life. At this point the coaddict may be so depressed, hostile, or anxious that he or she is completely out of control.

RELAPSE PREVENTION FOR THE FAMILY

While each family member is responsible for his or her own recovery and no one can recover for another, the symptoms of addiction and coaddiction each impact upon the relapse potential of the other. Even if the alcoholic is no longer drinking and no longer experiencing the drinking-related symptoms of the disease, the post acute withdrawal symptoms affect and are affected by coaddiction. Both the symptoms of post acute withdrawal and the symptoms of coaddiction are stress sensitive. Stress intensifies the symptoms and the symptoms intensify stress. As a result, the recovering addict and the coaddict can become a stress generating team that unknowingly and unconsciously complicates each other's recovery and creates a high risk of relapse.

What can family members do to reduce the risk of their own relapse and the risk of relapse in the recovering addict? They can become informed about the addictive disease, recovery, and the symptoms that accompany recovery. They must recognize that the symptoms of post acute withdrawal are sobriety-based symptoms of addiction rather than character defects, emotional disturbances, or mental illness. At the same time they must accept and recognize the symptoms of coaddiction and become involved in Al-Anon and/or personal therapy as they develop plans for their own recovery.

Clinical experience with relapse prevention planning in a variety of treatment programs has indicated that the family can be a powerful ally in preventing relapse in the addict. In 1980, relapse prevention planning was modified to include the involvement of significant others including family members. This significantly increased effectiveness. With further clinical experience, however, other problems became apparent. Many family members refused to participate in relapse prevention planning. Other family members participated in a manner that was counterproductive.

In 1983 relapse prevention planning was expanded to include relapse prevention in both the addicted person and the coaddict. The newly designed relapse prevention planning protocol utilizes the family's motivation to get the addict sober. As family members become involved in relapse prevention planning, a strong focus is placed on coaddiction and its role in family relapse. Family members are helped to recognize their own coaddiction and become actively involved in their own treatment. Addiction is presented as a family disease that affects all family members requiring them to get treatment.

All members of an addicted family are prone to return to self-defeating behaviors that can cause them to become out of control. An acute relapse episode can occur with an addict or a coaddict family member. Like addicts who develop serious problems even though they never use alcohol or drugs, the coaddict often becomes dysfunctional even though the addict is sober and working an active recovery program.

It is important to protect the family from the stress that may be generated by the symptoms of post acute withdrawal experienced by the recovering person and to cooperate in plans to protect the recovering person from stress created by symptoms of coaddiction. Remember that none of you became ill overnight. Recovery will, likewise, take place over a long period of time. Develop a plan to prevent personal relapse and support relapse prevention plans for the recovering addict.

Family Relapse Prevention Planning is intended to help prevent acute relapse episodes in the recovering addict, to prevent crisis in the coaddict, to develop a relapse prevention plan for both the addict and coaddict and to develop an early intervention plan to interrupt acute relapse episodes in both the recovering addict and the coaddict. For the addict this involves interrupting problems that are caused both by the Post Acute Withdrawal (PAW) Syndrome in the sober addict and by alcohol or drug use in the addict who has returned to drinking or using. For the coaddict this involves interrupting the coaddiction crisis. The family needs to work with a counselor to establish a formal relapse prevention plan that will allow them to support each other's recovery and to help intervene if the relapse warning symptoms get out of control.

The family relapse prevention planning protocol consists of twelve basic procedures. These are:

1. **Stabilization:** The first step in relapse prevention planning is to stabilize both the addict and the coaddict. The addict is stabilized through the process of detoxification or treatment of post acute withdrawal symptoms. The spouse is stabilized by treating the coaddict crisis, through detachment from the addict crisis, by regaining a reality-based perspective, and the development of some basic personal strengths. This often requires both attendance at Al-Anon and professional counseling.

2. **Assessment:** Prior to developing a relapse prevention plan it is necessary to evaluate the addict, the coaddicts, and the family system. The evaluation should assess the current problems of each family member, their willingness and ability to initiate a personal recovery program, and their willingness to become involved in a program of family recovery.

3. **Education About Alcoholism, Coaddiction, and Relapse:** Accurate information is the most powerful of all recovery tools. The addict and the family must learn about the disease of addiction, the condition of coaddiction, treatment, and relapse prevention planning. This education is best provided to the family as a unit in multiple family classes. It is helpful if the education is accompanied by separate group therapy programs for each family member. The addict should enter an addict group, the adult coaddict should enter a spouse's group, and the coaddict children should enter a children's group. It is in these group treatment sessions that individual recovery of all family members is initiated.

4. **Warning Sign Identification:** Both the addict and the coaddict need to identify the personal warning signs that indicate that they are becoming dysfunctional. Again, this is best done in a group setting. The addict is better able to identify relapse warning signs when working with other addicts. Coaddicts are best able to initially identify relapse warning signs when working with other coaddicts. Re-

lapse warning sign lists for addiction and coaddiction are useful guides for personal warning sign identification.

5. **Family Validation of Warning Signs:** After each family member has developed a personal list of warning signs and reviewed these in his or her group, a series of family sessions is scheduled. During these sessions all family members present their personal lists of warning signs and ask for feedback. Other family members discuss the warning signs, help assess if they are specific and observable. New warning signs may be added to the list based upon the feedback of others. Since each family member has a list of warning signs that precede acute relapse episodes there is no identified patient. All participate from a position of equality. They essentially say to each other, "We have all been equally affected, in various ways, by addictive disease."

6. **The Family Relapse Prevention Plan:** Family members discuss each of their warning signs, how the family has dealt with those warning signs in the past, and what strategies could be effectively used in the future. Future situations in which the warning signs are likely to be encountered are identified. Strategies for more effective management of the warning signs for each family member are discussed. During this process a great deal of role playing and problem solving occurs. Problems are often identified that are taken back to the separate therapy groups for further work.

7. **Inventory Training:** All members of the family receive training in how to complete a morning planning inventory and an evening review inventory. These focus heavily on time structuring, realistic goal setting, and problem solving.

8. **Communication Training:** The family members must learn to communicate effectively in order for RPP to work. The family is trained in the process of giving and receiving feedback in a constructive and caring manner.

9. **Review of the Recovery Program:** All family members will report to the family the recovery program that they have established for themselves. The focus here is, "How will you and I know that I am doing well in my recovery?" All are invited to express their recovery needs and point out their progress in treatment.

10. **Denial Interruption Plan:** Both addiction and co-addiction are diseases of denial. Most of the denial is unconscious. Neither the addict nor the coaddict realize that they are in denial when it is happening. It is important to take the reality of denial into account early. Each family member should be asked the question, "What are other people in your family supposed to do if they give you feedback about concrete warning signs and you deny it, ignore the feedback, or become angry and upset?" Each family member should recommend specific plans

for dealing with their own denial. This open discussion sets the stage for intervention should denial become a problem in the future.

11. **The Relapse Early Intervention Plan:** Addiction and coaddiction are prone to relapse. Relapse means becoming dysfunctional in recovery. For the recovering addict relapse may involve alcohol and drug use, or it may simply mean that the person becomes so depressed, anxious, angry, or upset that he is dysfunctional in sobriety. For the coaddict relapse means the return to a state of coaddict crisis that interferes with normal functioning. Once family members enter an acute relapse episode they are out of control of their thoughts, emotions, judgments, and behavior. They often need the direct help of other family members to interrupt the crisis. Many times they resist this help. They act as if they do not want help even though they desperately need it. The family is instructed in the process of intervention. Intervention is a method of helping people who refuse to be helped. This intervention training has resulted in a radical decrease in the duration and severity of relapse episodes in family members.

12. **Follow-up and Reinforcement:** Addiction and coaddiction are life-long conditions. The symptoms can go into remission but they never totally disappear. They rest quietly, waiting for a lapse in the recovery program to become active again. It is important that the family

maintain an ongoing recovery program including AA, Al-Anon, and periodic relapse prevention checkups with a professional addiction counselor.

Chapter X

THE RELAPSE PREVENTION SELF-HELP GROUP

Relapse prevention is a way of life. The recognition and interruption of relapse symptoms must become a daily habit. As with any habit, relapse prevention is difficult to maintain. Many relapse prone persons find that they need support to keep their relapse prevention plan working. They have found that meeting with others who are relapse prone is helpful. They set up regular meetings to discuss their relapse prevention plans and to exchange information.

In some areas these relapse prevention self-help groups have been incorporated in AA meetings. In other places special AA meetings have emerged for relapse prone alcoholics. These meetings are often called "Golden Slippers Meetings."

Some AA members discuss their progress with relapse prevention planning during regular AA meetings. Since they have integrated relapse prevention planning into their regular twelve-step AA recovery program this is usually not a problem.

Some AA groups, however, are reluctant to discuss relapse prevention during formal AA meetings. Although relapse prevention planning is completely compatible with the AA program, it is not a part of that program. The method itself and literature such as this manual have not been conference approved. As a result many AA meetings do not allow discussion of the relapse prevention planning methods.

As a result, some recovering persons have developed relapse prevention self-help groups that are independent of but cooperative with AA and other Twelve Step Groups. These persons do not stop going to AA; they simply start going to an additional self-help meeting that focuses specifically on their problems with preventing relapse.

The Relapse Prevention Self-Help Group is a structured meeting that is designed to assist relapse prone persons suffering from addictive disease to recognize the warning signs of relapse and to learn how to effectively manage these symptoms.

The group is designed as a voluntary self-help organization. There are no dues, fees, or memberships required. The primary purpose of the group is to help relapse prone individuals recognize their unique problems and to meet together to give mutual help and support in times of crisis.

The Relapse Prevention Self-Help Group is designed to work in cooperation with Alcoholics Anonymous and related programs. It is also designed to work cooperatively with professional counseling. The Relapse Prevention Self-Help Group is not designed as a substitute or replacement for AA or professional counseling.

The only qualification for membership in the Relapse Prevention Self-Help Group is a history of honest attempts at sobriety that have failed or a fear that relapse may occur. The Relapse Prevention Self-Help Groups recognize that relapse prone individuals have experienced many failures in recovery. Their history of failure often leads them to be labeled or stigmatized as failures. Because of the unique problems that go hand and hand with a long history of failure at recovery, the relapse prone person needs a special support group in which to find the fellowship of other recovering persons who have experienced a similar history of failure.

Many warning signs may develop without the conscious knowledge or intent of the relapse prone person. As a result, the Relapse Prevention Self-Help Group is designed to provide feedback to the members about the symptoms that are being observed by other group members. The major factors that make RPP self-help groups so effective are: daily inventories that identify warning signs early, efforts to stop the warning signs before they get out of control, talking openly and honestly about the warning signs and what you are doing to stop them with others, and listening to feedback from others.

It has been the experience of people involved in Relapse Prevention Self-Help Groups that there are no hopeless alcoholics. Recovery is possible even for persons with long histories of chronic relapse and chronic failures at recovery. The key to recovery is a combination of professional treatment, self-help group involvement based upon the twelve steps of AA, and the special steps of relapse prevention planning.

AA tells us that recovery is possible by following twelve basic steps. (179) (182) Relapse prevention planning (RPP) builds on these steps. RPP suggests that there are pathways to successful recovery and pathways to relapse. The pathway to successful recovery can be described in a Developmental Model of Recovery. The pathways to relapse can be described in terms of partial recovery and the phases and warning signs of relapse.

AA tells us that some people seem to be "constitutionally incapable" of recovery. RPP tells us that by studying these people and determining what is happening to them physically, psychologically, socially, and spiritually, we can figure out what needs to happen in order for them to become "constitutionally capable of recovery." AA provides twelve steps to recovery. RPP applies them in a special manner to those who are relapse prone.

The First Step tells us to admit that we are powerless over alcohol, that our lives have become unmanageable. RPP teaches that we are not only powerless over alcohol, but also over long-term withdrawal symptoms that follow us into recovery. RPP also describes "unmanageable living" with the concept of "behavioral compulsion." Life will remain unmanageable as long as we turn to obsessive or compulsive behaviors to avoid dealing with ourselves, our thinking, our emotions, and our actions.

The Second Step tells us to believe that a power greater than ourselves can restore us to sanity. This step suggests that we are insane to be using alcohol and drugs. RPP describes a sobriety-based insanity in terms of post acute withdrawal, addictive thinking, addictive mistaken beliefs, and an addictive social system that keeps mistaken beliefs alive.

RPP affirms the Second Step promise of the possibility of recovery. It also confirms that recovery cannot come exclusively from within the relapse prone person because awareness is too distorted by addictive thinking and mistaken addictive beliefs. They must come to believe that they cannot do it alone, but that there is effective help available. There is a power that provides that strength and courage to find and utilize knowledge and methods to develop the discipline needed for recovery.

The Third Step tells us to make a decision to turn our wills and our lives over to the care of God as we understand Him. When this step is applied to relapse prevention planning it means surrendering to the will of God in utilizing new information and going through the discipline of completing a relapse prevention plan.

The Fourth Step tells us to take a fearless and searching moral inventory of ourselves. RPP suggests a specialized inventory based on the symptoms of PAW, the symptoms of partial recovery, and the warning signs of relapse that indicate that PAW is out of control. This specialized inventory focuses on evaluating your own pattern of relapse.

The Fifth Step tells us to admit to God, to ourselves, and to another human being the exact nature of our wrongs. In terms of RPP, it is not enough to personally know what your warning signs are. You must discuss these warning signs at AA meetings, in group therapy, with your AA sponsor, therapist, and family members. RPP further encourages you to get involved in a Relapse Prevention Self-Help Group that involves key friends, family members, and members of AA. The more people who are familiar with your warning signs and can help you recognize them and stop them the better off you will be.

The Sixth Step tells us to become entirely ready to have God remove all these defects of character. In RPP character defects are broken down into three categories.

The first category involves the symptoms of neurological damage (Post Acute Withdrawal) caused by chronic addictive use. These symptoms require time plus proper nutrition and stress management in order to heal. The second category involves addictive thinking and addictive mistaken beliefs that create discomfort in recovery. Self-defeating thought and belief patterns must be identified by talking to others and being open to feedback from others. The third category involves problems with thinking and living that interfere with spiritual growth and development.

RPP suggests that it is helpful to categorize and accurately label character defects. Each different type of defect requires a different approach in order to correct it. This need for different approaches to different types of problems was suggested by Father Martin when he said, "If I get hit by a truck, take me to a hospital; don't take me to church or to an AA meeting. While I'm in the hospital I'll use the AA principles to give me strength to get through the treatment."

RPP suggests that we must become willing to recover from the physical and neurological damage of our addiction as well as the psychological (thinking, feeling, and acting) damage. This process is made possible through a program of spiritual growth that provides the strength and hope to persist in recovery without the need to turn to addictive use.

Step Seven suggests that we humbly ask God to remove our shortcomings. God created an orderly universe. Addiction destroys that order in a person's life. But God has also created a process of restoring order. RPP suggests that there is a pathway to recovery. It is not easy, but it is there. By learning what that pathway is and asking for the strength to follow it, all three types of character defects will be removed with time.

A man was drowning in a flood and he prayed for God to save him. A man on shore threw him a rope, but he refused to grab it saying, "God will save me." He was swept from shore and a boat pulled up near him and someone threw him a life preserver. He refused to take hold of it saying, "God will save me." Finally as he was being drawn into swift rapids, a helicopter hovered overhead and someone dangled a rope in front of him. The man yelled, "No, thank you, God will save me." He then plunged to his death. A few minutes later he stood before God. He was angry because God let him down and he said, "God why didn't you save me?" God said, "What did you expect me to do? First I sent a man with a rope, then I sent a boat, and finally I sent a helicopter. You refused my help all three times."

To be willing to have God remove all of these defects we must realize that God often works through other people. God often removes our defects of character by sending us to a good physician, nutritional counselor, alcoholism counselor, clergyman, or AA member. He always gives us a choice. We always have the right to say, "No thank you. I won't do that."

Step Eight suggests that we make a list of all the persons we have harmed and become willing to make amends to them all. In other words, we need to get ready to clean house. We need to prepare to straighten out our past relationships. Step 8 tells us to identify those we have harmed, how we have harmed them, and become ready to make amends. Relapse prone people tend to have longer lists of people to whom they need to make amends. This is because so many people have been hurt in the long process of short-term abstinence followed by relapse.

Step Nine suggests that we actually make amends to such people wherever possible except when to do so would injure them or others. RPP affirms the need to straighten out our past relationships. It is important in preventing relapse to recognize that this step is listed as number nine for a reason. To try to make amends too soon can create so much stress and pain that it can induce relapse.

Step Ten tells us to continue to take personal inventory and when we are wrong promptly admit it. RPP suggests a special form of daily inventory composed of a morning planning inventory and an evening review inventory. RPP suggests that we acknowledge relapse warning signs promptly and take action to do something about them. The longer a warning sign is left alone the more likely it is to grow in intensity until it becomes so powerful that it leads back to addictive use. Recognize the warning sign, admit it is there, and use relapse prevention planning to manage it.

Step Eleven tells us to seek through prayer and meditation to improve our conscious contact with God as we understand Him, praying only for knowledge of His will and the power to carry that out. Prayer and meditation will provide a source of inspiration and courage to reach for and accept help. In prayer and meditation we will find the strength to try again for recovery.

Step Twelve suggests that, having had a spiritual awakening, we try to carry this message to alcoholics and to practice these principles in all our affairs. Repeated relapse interferes with spiritual growth. Continuous sobriety or longer periods of sobriety allow for growth that motivates those who have experienced a spiritual awakening to share their knowledge of relapse prevention planning with other relapse prone addicts.

RPP suggests that relapse prone addicts have special needs, but that there is hope for recovery. The fact that one relapse prone person can recover is a primary source of hope for others who are still struggling to do so. But more than hope is needed. There is the need to transmit knowledge, skills, and personal support as a person struggles to learn this new knowledge and put the new skills to work. As a result, RPP strongly recommends group therapy and relapse prevention self-help groups as primary vehicles of learning about relapse prevention planning. When this is coupled with the principles and practices of AA, a powerful formula for recovery results.

MEETING FORMAT

The Relapse Prevention Self-Help Group Meeting will follow a standard format consisting of the following:

1. ***The Opening Statement:*** The meeting will be opened with the chairperson announcing the name of the meeting, introducing himself or herself, and welcoming all people who are attending. The chairperson will then designate a member of the meeting to read the introduction statement* for the Relapse Prevention Self-Help Group. The chairperson will then ask another group member to read the basic tools of the Relapse Prevention Self-Help Group.

*See appendix.

2. ***A Quiet Time:*** A brief period of two to three minutes of silence will then be called to allow people to relax, clear their minds, and prepare themselves to benefit from the content of the meeting. During this period a brief relaxation exercise may be used such as instructing the people to take a deep breath, hold it for a moment and slowly exhale. The goal here is for all members to get themselves in a frame of mind where they can benefit from the meeting.
3. ***Reading of the Topic Material:*** The chairperson will be responsible for selecting a topic for discussion. Each topic is to have material which can be read to the group in three to five minutes. The reading of the topic will set the stage for a speaker.
4. ***The Speaker:*** The chairperson will also be responsible for finding a speaker who must be a relapse prone individual who has achieved a significant period of recovery. This speaker will have the assignment of discussing his or her personal experiences with the information that is part of the daily topic. The speaker is encouraged to share his or her personal experiences with situations pertaining to the topic material. The lead presentation should take no longer than fifteen to twenty minutes.
5. ***Break:*** A brief break will be announced. During the break there will be decaffeinated coffee, decaffeinated cola beverages, and if snacks are available they will ***not*** consist of sweets or refined carbohydrates. The snacks could include peanuts, fruits, or cheeses. It

is important that the Relapse Prevention groups recognize that caffeine and sugars can create adverse mood states that can trigger relapse warning signs.

During this break members will be encouraged to introduce themselves to other members they don't know and to exchange phone numbers.

6. ***Comments:*** When the group reconvenes members will have a chance to comment on the topic, the lead speaker's presentation, or any other issues they choose to discuss in the group. It is the responsibility of the chairperson to ensure that all persons have an opportunity to comment, and that their comments are contained to a period not longer than 3 to 5 minutes. When a person comments it is the responsibility of other group members to listen. Questioning, confrontation, and feedback to the people making comments are not allowed during the comment period of the meeting.
7. ***The Feedback Session:*** The final segment of the meeting will be the feedback session. Individual group members who would like to present information about their own recovery and receive feedback from other group members will be encouraged to do so. Persons requesting feedback are to briefly present the area of their recovery that they would like to receive feedback on from the group. The group will then have an opportunity to ask them clarifying questions. This will be done in the structured format where every member of the group will have an opportunity to ask questions

to clarify what they have heard. After everyone has had an opportunity to ask questions, the chairperson will go around the circle again and ask anyone who is willing to give feedback to the person to do so.

Feedback consists of four things: 1) What I think about what the person said, 2) What I felt while the person was talking, 3) The strengths I see in the person's recovery program that will help them get well, and 4) The weaknesses I see in the person's recovery program that may be setting him or her up to drink or use addictively.

It is important that anyone requesting feedback do so in a strictly voluntary fashion. No one is to be coerced to ask for feedback. It is also important that members of the group who give feedback practice rigorous honesty while learning how to be supportive. The goal is to support others while pointing out weaknesses in their recovery programs which may cause them problems.

8. ***Adjournment:*** The chairperson will announce the time and place of the next meeting, recruit a speaker for the next meeting, and adjourn the meeting.
9. ***Duration of the Meeting:*** The typical Relapse Prevention Self-Help Group Meeting will be two hours in duration. The meeting introduction and quiet time should take approximately 15 minutes. The reading of the lead topic and the presentation of the lead speaker should take approximately 30 minutes. The commenting period should take approximately 30 to

40 minutes. The feedback session should be limited to approximately 40 minutes. No more than two individuals will have an opportunity to receive feedback per group session. There should be a mandatory time limit on feedback of 20 minutes maximum.

FINAL WORD

Imagine that you are on a hiking trip in the middle of the desert. You see a figure in the distance. It is an old man bearded and half naked, on hands and knees, with his fingers clawing at the sandy earth. You ask, "What are you doing?" "I'm digging for buried treasure," says the old man. "How long have you been at it?" you ask. "Weeks—months maybe, It is hard and slow work." You notice the old man's bloody fingers and his raw and calloused knuckles. You say, "Listen, man! Digging with your bare hands is a pretty inefficient method. That hole is only a couple of feet deep. Let me loan you my shovel." You reach into your backpack, pull out a lightweight, tempered-edge spade, and drive it into the ground. In less than five minutes you have demonstrated to the old fellow that more progress can be made in moments than he could make in a month of using his bare hands.

Then an amazing thing happens. The old man's eyes fill with hate and his face flushes angrily. He charges at you, grabs the shovel from your hands, and throws it away. "Get away from me with your new fangled contraptions," he says. "I've been digging this way all of my life and it works fine. Now you just get out of here and leave me alone. I'll be fine doing it my way."

Many people seek recovery from addictive disease in the same way that this old man is digging for treasure. They attempt to maintain sobriety without the tools of AA or professional treatment. If digging with your bare hands is the only way you know to get the job done, you do it that way. But it is slow and hard work, and the chances of finding treasure in the form of long-term, comfortable, sobriety are very low.

AA is a tool for recovery much like a shovel is a tool in searching for treasure. A shovel gives you a better and more efficient way to dig. Having a shovel does not guarantee that you will find what you are looking for, but it sure does increase your chances and it makes the process of searching for it much easier and more enjoyable.

Back in 1935 the founders of AA provided hope by showing alcoholics that recovery was possible. They provided a shovel in the form of 12 steps that for many has led to recovery. Since 1935 a lot has been learned about recovery. The basic principles of AA have proven to be accurate. There is treasure in the form of long-term, comfortable sobriety. It can be found by digging exactly where the twelve steps tell you to dig and by using the shovel it has provided to make the task easier.

But let us go back to our old digger. Suppose he takes the shovel you offer him. But suppose that after awhile he comes to rock that the shovel cannot penetrate. You offer him a pick ax and once again his goal becomes attainable. Professional treatment and AA together provide the pick and shovel necessary for large numbers of people to reach the goal of sobriety.

But what of the many many people who have used their hands, used the shovel and the pick, and still have hit gigantic boulders that cannot be removed with the tools they have. Relapse prevention planning provides an air hammer—if you choose to use it.

Having the proper tools does not remove your responsibility to use your hands and dig in the right place. The right tools just let you get farther faster if you choose to work at it. It also does not guarantee that you will find long-term, comfortable sobriety. But it does increase your chances.

Relapse prevention planning does not replace AA nor professional treatment, nor does it diminish the importance of AA principles and practices. It simply adds another powerful recovery tool to the already powerful principles of AA.

Nor is this model of relapse prevention planning the end of the story. The shovel, pick ax, and air hammer made vast improvements in how fast and well people could dig. But people kept looking for better ways. And soon the backhoe and the steam shovel were invented. It is our hope that this book has removed some of the fear and threat from the idea of relapse.

It is our strong belief that ignorance is the major enemy of every recovering person. The more we learn about addictive disease, the more effective we can be in treating it and working toward recovery. This book has been an effort to turn on the lights of your mind. The blind fear of relapse is no longer necessary. As we understand more about the relapse process we can recognize with more and more clarity what is necessary to avoid relapse. We can replace wishful thinking with scientifically known facts.

Remember, this book is not a final answer. It is rather a crude beginning. There is much more to be learned. There are many more personal experiences to analyze and learn from. New research is rapidly becoming available. We may learn something new tomorrow that could greatly improve these methods. Our goal is to learn more about this illness so that chemically dependent people who are now condemned to death may learn how to live.

It is our sincere hope that this book has been helpful. But remember, knowledge alone is not enough. That knowledge must be put into action. Take this new knowledge and these principles into your recovery programs.

Carry the message into AA and to your families and to other suffering alcoholics. Start relapse prevention groups that can make relapse prone people feel comfortable and at home. Most importantly, offer support and hope rather than judgment to other relapse prone people. We sincerely hope that the people reading this book will be stirred into action; that they will begin to study and research and learn how to cope with America's #1 killer—Addictive Disease.

Appendix

The Relapse Prevention Self-Help Group Introduction

The Relapse Prevention Self-Help Group is a structured meeting that is designed to assist relapse prone alcoholics and chemically dependent people to recognize the warning signs and symptoms of relapse and to learn how to effectively manage these signs and symptoms. The group is designed as a voluntary selfhelp organization. There are no dues, fees, or memberships required. The primary purpose of the group is to help relapse prone individuals to recognize their unique problems and to form together to give mutual help and support in times of crisis.

The Relapse Prevention Self-Help Group is designed to work in cooperation with Alcoholics Anonymous and related programs. It is also designed to work cooperatively with professional counseling. The Relapse Prevention Self-Help Group is not designed as a substitute or replacement for AA or other forms of professional counseling.

The only qualification for membership in the Relapse Prevention Self-Help Group is a history of honest attempts at sobriety that have failed or a current fear of relapsing. The Relapse Prevention Self-Help Groups recognize that relapse prone individuals have experienced many failures at recovery. Their history of failure often leads them to be labeled or stigmatized as failures. Because of the unique problems that go hand in hand with a long history of failure at recovery, the relapse prone persons need a special support group where they can find the fellowship of other recovering persons who have experienced a similar history of failure.

Relapse is a progressive process that is marked by definite, predictable, and progressive warning signs. Once relapse prone persons become aware of their personal warning signs, they can create a relapse prevention plan that will allow them to successfully manage these warning signs of relapse. Many warning signs may develop without the conscious knowledge or intent of the relapse prone person. As a result the Relapse Prevention Self-Help Group is designed to provide feedback to the members about the warning signs and symptoms that are being observed by other group members. It is through this process of daily inventory, management of warning signs, and constant self disclosure and feedback from others that relapse can be prevented.

It has been the experience of people involved in the Relapse Prevention Self-Help group that there is no such thing as a hopeless alcoholic. Recovery is possible even for persons with long histories of chronic relapse and chronic failures at recovery. The key to recovery is a combination of professional treatment, self-help group involvement based upon the twelve steps of AA, and the special steps of relapse prevention planning described by the Relapse Prevention Self-Help Group.

BIBLIOGRAPHY

ALCOHOLISM

In the past fifteen years a great deal of new information has been learned about alcoholism. These references summarize the recent advances for those interested in technical research support for and general information about the concepts in this book.

1. Johnson, Vernon E., ***I'll Quit Tomorrow.*** New York, Harper & Row, 1973.
2. Kinney, Jean, and Leaton, Gwen, ***Loosening the Grip.*** St. Louis, Mo., C. V. Mosby Co., 1978.
3. Kissin, Benjamin and Begleiter, Henri, ***The Biology of Alcoholism, Volume 6, The Pathogenesis of Alcoholism—Psychosocial Factor.*** New York, Plenum Press, 1983.
4. Kissin, Benjamin and Begleiter, Henri, ***The Biology of Alcoholism. Volume 7, The Pathogenesis of Alcoholism—Biological Factors.*** New York, Plenum Press, 1983.
5. Miller, M., Gorski, T., Miller, D., ***Learning to Live Again.*** Independence, Mo., Independence Press, 1980.
6. Milam, James and Ketcham, Katherine, ***Under, the Influence—A Guide to the Myths and Realities of Alcoholism.*** Seattle, Washington, Madrona Publishers, 1981.
7. Pattison, E. Mansell and Kaufman, Edward, ***Encyclopedic Handbook of Alcoholism.*** New York, Gardner Press, 1982.
8. Royce, James E., ***Alcohol Problems and Alcoholism—A Comprehensive Survey.*** New York, The Free Press, 1981.
9. U.S. Department of Health and Human Services, ***First Special Report to Congress on Alcohol and Health.*** National Institute on Alcohol Abuse and Alcoholism, Rockville, Maryland, December, 1971.
10. U.S. Department of Health and Human Services, ***Second Special Report to Congress on Alcohol and Health.*** National Institute on Alcohol Abuse and Alcoholism, Rockville, Maryland, June, 1974.
11. U.S. Department of Health and Human Services, ***Third Special Report to Congress on Alcohol and Health.*** National Institute on Alcohol Abuse and Alcoholism, Rockville, Maryland, June, 1978.
12. U.S. Department of Health and Human Services, ***Fourth Special Report to Congress on Alcohol and Health.*** National Institute on Alcohol Abuse and Alcoholism, Rockville, Maryland, January, 1981.
13. U.S. Department of Health and Human Services, ***Fifth Special Report to Congress on Alcohol and Health.*** National Institute on Alcohol Abuse and Alcoholism, Rockville, Maryland, December, 1983.

DISEASE CONCEPT

Alcoholism is widely accepted as a disease. The following are the primary references used to support the disease model of alcoholism.

14. Davies, D. L., Definitional Issues in Alcoholism. In ***Alcoholism: Interdisciplinary Approaches to An Enduring Problem,*** R. E. Tarter & A.A. Sugerman (Eds). Reading, Mass., Addison-Wesley, 1976.
15. Glatt, M. M., "The Question of Moderate Drinking Despite Loss of Control." ***British Journal of Addiction,*** 1976, 71, 135–144.
16. Glatt, M. M., "Alcoholism Disease Concept and Loss of Control Revisited." ***British Journal of Addiction,*** 1976, 71, 135–144.
17. Jellinek, E. M , ***The Disease Concept of Alcoholism.*** New Haven, Conn., College and University Press, in association with Hillhouse Press, New Brunswick, N.J., 1960.
18. Keller, M., "On the Loss of Control Phenomena in Alcoholism." ***British Journal of Addiction,*** 1972, 67, 153–166.
19. Knott, David H., M.D., Ph.D., ***Alcohol Problems Diagnosis and Treatment.*** New York. Pergamon Press, 1986.
20. Milam, James, ***The Emergent Comprehensive Concept of Alcoholism.*** Kirkland, Wa., ACA Press.
21. Milam, James A. and Ketchum, Katherine, ***Under the Influence—A Guide to the Myths and Realities of Alcoholism.*** Seattle, Washington, Madrona Publishers, 1981.
22. Rush, B., An inquiry into the effects of ardent spirits upon the human body and mind; with an account of the means of preventing and of the remedies for curing them, (1785?). Brookfield, Mass., Merriam (8th edn.)

There is not universal support for the disease concept of addictive disease. The major critiques of the disease model focus upon the failure, in the above original sources, to integrate a bio-psycho social concept. There is also concern that some problem drinkers do not have an addictive disease per se and the disease model either ignores or inappropriately labels and treats these individuals. The following are the primary references that critique the disease model of alcoholism.

23. Maisto, S. A., & Scheftt, B. K., The Constructs for Cravings for Alcohol and Loss of Control Drinking: Help or Hindrance to Research. In ***Addictive Behaviors,*** 1977, 2, 207–217.
24. Marlatt, G. A., Craving for Alcohol, Loss of Control, and Relapse: A Cognitive-Behavioral Analysis. In ***Alcoholism: New Directions in Behavioral Research and Treatment,*** Nathan, P. E., Marlatt, G. A and Lobers T. (eds.). New York, Plenum, 1978.
25. Mello, N. K , Behavioral Studies in Alcoholism. In ***The Biology of Alcoholism (Vol 2),*** B. Kissin and H. Begleiter (eds.). New York, Plenum, 1972.
26. Pattison, E. M., Sobell, M. B., Sobell, L. C. (eds.), ***Emerging Concepts of Alcohol Dependence.*** New York, Springer, 1977.
27. Robinson, D., "The Alcohologist's Addiction: Some Implications of Having Lost Control Over the Disease Concept of Alcoholism." ***Quarterly Journal of Studies on Alcohol,*** 1972, 32, 1028–1042.

ALCOHOLISM AND GENETICS

It has been demonstrated that the transmission of alcoholism is genetically influenced. Current research is pursuing the question, What factors are influenced genetically that produce an increased susceptibility to alcoholism? The following articles summarize the recent research.

28. Goodwin, Donall, ***Is Alcoholism Hereditary?*** New York, Oxford University Press, 1976.
29. Goodwin, D, W., "Genetics of Alcoholism, Substance and Alcohol Actions/Misuse." ***Clinical Science Review:*** 1:101–117, 1980.
30. Grove, William M., & Cadoret, Remi J., Genetic Factors in Alcoholism. In ***The Biology of Alcoholism, Volume 7, The Pathogenesis of Alcoholism—Biological Factors,*** Kissin, Benjamin and Begleiter, Henri, (eds.). New York, Plenum Press, 1983.
31. Leiber, C. S,, "The Metabolism of Alcohol," ***Scientific American.*** March 1976.
32. Leiber, C. S., Hasumara, Y., Teschke, P., Matsuzaki, S., and Korsten, M., "The Effect of Chronic Ethanol Consumption on Acetaldehyde Metabolism," in ***The Role of Acetaldehyde in the Actions of Ethanol,*** ed, K. 0. Lindros and C. J. P. Ericksson (Helsinki: Finnish Foundation for Alcohol Studies, Vol. 23, 1975).
33. Leiber, C. S., and Dicarli, L. M., "The Role of the Hepatic Microsomal Ethanol Oxidizing System (MEOS) for Ethanol Metabolism in Vivo," ***Journal of Pharmacology and Experimental Therapeutics,*** Vol. 181 (1972).
34. Schuckit, Marc A., and Rayses, V., "Ethanol Ingestion: Differences in Blood Acetaldehyde Concentrations in Relatives of Alcoholics and Controls," ***Science,*** Vol. 203 (1979).
35. Shuckitt, Mark A., Li Ting Kai, Clonninger, C. Robert Deitrich, Richard A., "The Genetics of Alcoholism—A Summary of the Proceedings of a Conference Convened at the University of California, Davis." Reported in ***Alcoholism: Clinical and Experimental Research,*** Vol. 9, No. 6, pg. 475–492, November/December 1985.
36. U.S. Department of Health and Human Services, ***Fifth Special Report to the U.S. Congress on Alcohol and Health from the Secretary of Health and Human Services.*** National Institute on Alcohol Abuse and Alcoholism, Rockville, Maryland, December, 1983. Pgs. 15–24.
37. US Journal of Drug and Alcohol Dependence, Alcohol Tolerance Different in CoA Men, A news story in ***The US Journal of Drug and Alcohol Dependence,*** Vol. 9. No 12, pg. 12, December, 1985.
38. US Journal of Drug and Alcohol Dependence, Hyperactive Teens More Likely to Drink, A news story in ***The US Journal of Drug and Alcohol Dependence,*** Vol. 9, No. 12, pg 19, December, 1985.

STRESS MANAGEMENT AND ADDICTIVE DISEASE

Stress management and relaxation training have proven to be a useful adjunct in the treatment of addictive disease. The following articles describe the research basis and methodology for the use of stress management and relaxation training in treatment.

39. Engstrom, David R , and Liebert, David E., Muscle Tension and Experienced Control: Effects of Alcohol Intake Vs. Biofeedback on Alcoholics and Non-Alcoholics. In ***Currents in Alcoholism—Recent Advances in Research and Treatment (Vol. VII),*** Galanter, Marc (eds.). New York, Grune & Stratton, 1980. Pgs, 219–228.
40. Gorski, Terence T., and Troiani, Joseph E., ***Self Regulation/Biofeedback and Alcoholism—An Applied Model.*** Ingalls Memorial Hospital, Harvey, Illinois, October, 1978.

ADDICTIVE CHEMICALS

Chemical addictions involve dependence upon moodaltering drugs including alcohol. Although there is a common core addiction syndrome that pertains to all chemical addiction, each drug group has distinct effects during intoxication and withdrawal which need to be understood. The following references will aid in understanding these similarities and differences. These references describe biological, psychological, and social factors that are similar in addictive disease. Recent research on endorphins and enkephelons and their role in addictive disease is reviewed.

41. Bennett, Gerald, Vourakis, Christine, Woolf, Donna S., ***Substance Abuse—Pharmacologic, Developmental, and Clinical Perspectives.*** New York, Wiley Medical Publications, 1983.
42. Blum, Kenneth, ***Handbook of Abuseable Drugs.*** New York, Gardner Press, 1984.
43. Blum, Richard H. Bovet, Daniel, Moore, James, ***Controlling Drugs: International Handbook for Psychoactive Drug Classification.*** Jossey-Bass Publishers, 1974.
44. Cohen, G., & Collins, M. A., "Alkaloids from Catecholamines in Adrenal Tissue: Possible Role in Alcoholism," ***Science,*** Vol. 167 (1970).
45. David, Joe, ***Endorphins, New Waves in Brain Chemistry.*** Garden City, New York, Doubleday & Co., Inc., 1984.
46. Davis V. E., and Walsh, M. J., "Alcohol, Amines, Alkaloids: A Possible Biochemical Basis for Alcohol Addiction," ***Science,*** Vol. 167 (1970).
47. Hamilton, Helen Klusek, Rose, Minnie Bowen, Gever, Larry N., ***A Professional Guide to Drugs.*** Springhouse, Pennsylvania, Intermed Communications, Inc., 1982.
48. Keeley, Kim A. and Solomon, Joel, New Perspectives on the Similarities and Differences of Alcoholism and Drug Abuse. In ***Currents in Alcoholism, Recent Advances in Research and Treatment (Vol. VIII),*** Galanter, Marc (eds.). New York, Grune and Stratton, 1981, pp. 99118.

COMPULSIVE BEHAVIORS

Compulsive behaviors are actions that produce intense excitement, emotional release, or mood alteration and are followed by long-term pain or discomfort. These behaviors can be internal (thinking, imagining, feeling) or they can be external (working, playing, talking, etc.). Compulsive behaviors create biopsycho-social patterns that are similar to the core addiction syndrome that occurs with addictive chemicals. The following references provide an overview of a variety of compulsive behaviors and related research.

49. Carnes, Patrick, ***The Sexual Addiction.*** Minneapolis, Minnesota, Comp Care Publications, 1983.
50. Conway, Flo and Siegelman, Jim, ***Snapping: America's Epidemic of Sudden Personality Change.*** New York, J. B. Lippincott Company, 1978.
51. Friedman, Meyer and Resenman, Ray H., ***Type A Behavior and Your Heart.*** Greenwich, Connecticut, Fawcett Publications, 1974.
52. Friedman, Meyer and Ulmer, Diane, ***Treating Type A Behavior and Your Heart.*** New York, Alfred A. Knopf, 1984.
53. Glasser, William, ***Positive Addictions.*** New York, Harper and Row Publishers, 1976.
54. Hollis, Judi, ***Fat Is a Family Affair.*** Center City, Minnesota, The Hazelden Foundation, 1985.
55. Marlatt, G. Alan and Gordon, Judith R., ***Relapse Prevention—Maintenance Strategies in the Treatment of Addictive Behaviors.*** New York, Guilford Press, 1985.
56. Peele, Stanton, ***Love and Addiction.*** New York, Signet, May 1976, pp. 42–67.
57. Sargant, William, ***Battle for the Mind: A Physiology of Conversion and Brainwashing.*** New York, Harper & Row Publishers, 1957.
58. Stunkard, Albert J. and Stellar, Elliot (eds.), ***Eating and Its Disorders.*** Association for Research in Nervous and Mental Disease, Volume 62, New York, Raven Press, 1984.
59. Winn, Marie, ***The Plug in Drug: Television, Children, and the Family.*** New York, the Viking Press, 1977.

DENIAL IN ADDICTION

Addiction has been described as a disease of denial. Discussions of denial often include the concepts of compliance (consciously accepting the diagnosis while unconsciously resisting it) and surrender (conscious and unconscious acceptance). The typical treatment approach to denial is confrontation. The following references review original sources and recent updates to the concepts of denial, compliance, surrender, and confrontation.

60. Brown, Stephanie, ***Treating the Alcoholic, A Developmental Model of Recovery.*** New York, John Wiley & Sons, Inc., 1985. Pp. 58, 75–100.

61. Forrest, Gary G., ***Confrontation in Psychotherapy with the Alcoholic.*** Holmes Beach Florida, Learning Publications, Inc., 1982.
62. Gorski, Terence T., ***The Denial Process and Human Disease.*** Ingalls Memorial Hospital, May, 1976. Available from the CENAPS Corporation, P.O. Box 184, Hazel Crest, Illinois, 60429.
63. Gorski, Terence T., ***Denial Patterns: A System for Understanding the Alcoholic's Behavior.*** Ingalls Memorial Hospital, June, 1976. Available from the CENAPS Corporation, P.O. Box 184, Hazel Crest, Illinois, 60429.
64. Milam, James R. and Ketchum, Katherine, ***Under the Influence—A Guide to the Myths and Realities of Alcoholism.*** Seattle, Washington, Madrona Publishers, 1981, pp. 88–89.
65. Royce, James E., ***Alcohol Problems and Alcoholism-A Comprehensive Survey.*** New York, The Free Press of MacMillan Publishing Co., 1981, pp. 91–94.
66. Tiebout, Harry M., Psychological Factors Operating in Alcoholics Anonymous. In ***Current Therapies of Personality Disorders,*** B. Glueck (ed.) New York, Grune & Stratton, 1946, pp. 145–165.
67. Tiebout, Harry M., "Therapeutic Mechanisms of Alcoholics Anonymous," ***American Journal of Psychiatry,*** 1947, 100, 468–473.
68. Tiebout, Harry M., "The Act of Surrender in the Psychotherapeutic Process with Special Reference to Alcoholism," ***Quarterly Journal of Studies on Alcohol,*** 1949, 10, 48–58.
69. Tiebout, Harry M., "Surrender Versus Compliance in Therapy with Special Reference to Alcoholism," ***Quarterly Journal of Studies on Alcohol,*** 1953, 14, 5868.
70. Tiebout, Harry M., ***The Act of Surrender in the Therapeutic Process.*** New York, The National Council on Alcoholism, undated.
71. Tiebout, Harry M., "Conversion As a Psychological Phenomenon." Read before the New York Psychiatric Society, April 11, 1944. New York, National Council on Alcoholism, 1944.
72. Vaillant, George E., ***The Natural History of Alcoholism—Causes, Patterns, and Paths to Recovery.*** Cambridge, Massachusetts, Harvard University Press, 1983, pp. 31–32, 172–173.
73. Wallace, John, Working with the Preferred Defense Structure of the Recoverying Alcoholic. In ***Practical Approaches to Alcoholism Psychotherapy,*** S. Zimbers, J. Wallace and S. B. Blume (eds.). New York Plenum Press, 1978.
74. Zimberg, Sheldon, ***The Clinical Management of Alcoholism.*** New York, Brunner/Mazel Publishers, 1982, pp. 74–77, 110–115.

THE ADDICTIVE FAMILY

Addiction is typically described as a family disease. It is estimated that for each actively addicted person, three to five family members are seriously affected. Diagnostic and treatment approaches have matured in the past 15 years. The goal of family treatment has expanded from simply providing support for the alcoholic's recovery to identifying and providing positive treatment to affected family members. The following references review the concepts of enabling, family treatment, co-dependence, the adult children of alcoholics (ACOA) syndrome.

75. Ackerman, Robert J., ***Children of Alcoholics: A Guidebook for Educators, Therapists, and Parents.*** Holmes Beach, Florida, Learning Publications, 1978.
76. Black, Claudia, ***It Will Never Happen to Me.*** Denver, Colorado, MAC Printing and Publishing Division, 1982.
77. Carnes, Patrick, ***The Sexual Addiction.*** Minneapolis, Minnesota, Comp Care Publications, 1983, pp. 91–140.
78. Drews, Toby Rice, ***Getting Them Sober: A Guide for Those Who Live with an Alcoholic.*** Plainfield, New Jersey, Have Books, Logos International.
79. Dulfano, Celia, Family Therapy of Alcoholism. In ***Practical Approaches to Alcoholism Psychotherapy,*** S. Zimbers, J. Wallace and S. Blume. New York, Plenum Press, 1978, pp. 119–136.
80. Dulfano, Celia, ***Families, Alcoholism, and Recovery: Ten Stories.*** Hazelden Foundation, 1982.
81. Gorski, T., Miller, M., ***Focus on Family,*** "Relapse: The family's involvement," Parts I, II, III. Hollywood, Fl., ***The U.S. Journal of Drug and Alcohol Dependence, Inc.*** Sept./Oct., Nov./Dec., 1983, Jan./Feb., 1984.
82. Gorski, Terence T., ***Intimacy and Recovery—A Workshop Manual.*** Hazel Crest, Illinois, the CENAPS Corporation, 1984.
83. Gravitz, Herbert L. and Bowden, Julie D., ***Guide to Recovery: A Book for Adult Children of Alcoholics.*** Holmes Beach, Florida, Learning Publications, Inc., 1985.

84. Greenleaf, Jael, "Co-Alcoholic Para-Alcoholic: Who's Who and What's the Difference?" Presented at the National Council on Alcoholism, 1981 National Alcoholism Forum, New Orleans, Louisiana, April 12, 1981.
85. Howard, Donald P. and Howard, Nancy T., Treatment of the Significant Other. In ***Practical Approaches to Alcoholism Psychotherapy,*** S. Zimers, J. Wallace and S. Blume, New York, Plenum Press, 1978, pp. 137–162.
86. Kaufman, Edward and Kaufman, Pauline, ***Family Therapy of Drug and Alcohol Abuse.*** New York, 1979.
87. Miller, Merlene and Gorski, Terence T., ***Family Recovery: Growing Beyond Addiction.*** Independence, Missouri, Herald House Independence Press, 1982.
88. Norwood, Robin, ***Women Who Love Too Much.*** Los Angeles, Jeremy P. Tarcher, Inc., 1985.
89. Peele, Stanton, ***Love and Addiction.*** New York, Signet, May 1976.
90. Smith, Jan L., Gorski, Terence T., Miller, "Family Involvement in Relapse Prevention."—Course Handout, 1985.
91. Wegsheider, Sharon, ***Another Chance—Hope and Health for the Alcoholic Family.*** Palo Alto, California, Science and Behavior Books, Inc., 1983.
92. Woititz, Janet Geringer, ***Adult Children of Alcoholics.*** Pompano Beach, California, Health Communications, Inc., 1985.
93. Woititz, Janet Geringer, ***Struggle for Intimacy.*** Pompano Beach, California, Health Communications, Inc., 1985.

MORBIDITY AND MORTALITY OF ALCOHOLICS

Addictive disease shortens a person's life span by an estimated 11 years. There is evidence that, although sobriety does increase life expectancy, sober alcoholics remain at high risk for increased illness and premature death. The cause of death simply shifts from liver disease and other direct effects to cancer, heart disease and stress-related illness. The cause of death in sobriety reflect a strong impact of stress and toxin related diseases that may result from substitute chemical (caffeine and nicotine) and behavioral addictions.

94. Pell, S. and D'Alonzo, C. A., "A Five Year Mortality Study of Alcoholics," ***Journal of Occupational Medicine,*** 15:120–125, 1973.
95. Vaillant, George E., ***The Natural History of Alcoholism—Causes, Patterns, and Paths to Recovery.*** Cambridge, Massachusetts, Harvard University Press, 1983, pp. 161–173.

CAFFEINE

Research has identified caffeinism as a clinical syndrome characterized by intensified anxiety, apprehension and irritability as well as by physical symptoms of tachycardia and tremor. Although generally unrecognized, caffeine addiction may be a significant contributor to discomfort and dysfunction among persons recovering from addictive disease. Caffeine addiction may also be correlated with a return to addictive use in recovering persons.

96. Blattner, John F., ***The Effects of Caffeine Consumption with Recovering Alcoholics and its Relationship to Levels of Anxiety.*** An Unpublished Doctoral Dissertation, Prepared for the Fielding Institute, Santa Barbara, California, 1985.
97. Gilliland, K., Bullock, W., "Caffeine: A Potential Drug of Abuse," ***Advances in Alcohol and Substance Abuse,*** 1983, 3:53–73.
98. Dews, P. B., ***Caffeine, Perspective from Recent Research.*** New York, Springer-Verlag, 1984.
99. Gilliland, K., Bullock, W., "Caffeine: A Potential Drug of Abuse." In ***Addictive Behaviors,*** Shaffer, Howard and Stimmel. New York, Barry, Haworth Press, 1983, pp. 53–74.
100. Gilbert, R. M. "Caffeine As a Drug of Abuse." In ***Research Advances in Alcohol and Drug Problems, Vol. 3,*** Gibbons R. J., Israel Y. et al (eds.). New York, John Wiley and Sons, 1976.
101. Greden, J. F., "Anxiety or Caffeinism, A Diagnostic Dilemma." ***American Journal of Psychiatry,*** Vol. 131:1089–1092, 1974.
102. Greden, J. F., Fontaine P., Lubetsky, M. and Chamberlain, K., "Anxiety and Depression Associated with Caffeinism Among Psychiatric Patients," ***American Journal of Psychiatry,*** Vol. 135:963–966, 1978.
103. Nash, H., "Psychological Effects and Alcohol Antagonizing Properties of Caffeine," ***Quarterly Journal of Studies on Alcohol,*** Vol. 27:727–734, 1966.
104. Robertson, D., Frolich. J. C., Carr, R. K., Watson, J. T., Hollifield, J. W., Shand, D. C. and Oates, J. A., "Effects of Caffeine on Plasma Renin Activity, Catecholamines and High Blood Pressure," ***New England Journal of Medicine,*** Vol. 298:181–186, 1978.

POST ACUTE WITHDRAWAL

Recent research indicates that recovering alcoholics suffer from sub-clinical organic mental disorders that impair the ability to think, manage feelings and emotions, remember things, sleep restfully, maintain psychomotor coordination, and manage stress. This syndrome is chronic and persistent in early recovery for a period of 30–180 days. After that time symptoms intermittently recur, especially when a patient is under excessive stress, fatigued, and not well nourished. This syndrome has been described as post acute withdrawal, protracted withdrawal, dry drunk, and building up to drink. The following references document the presence, description, and hypothetical causes of this syndrome.

105. Abbott, M. W., and Gregson, R. A. M., Cognitive dysfunction in the prediction of relapse in alcoholics. J. Stud Alcohol 42:230–243, 1981.
106. Adams, K., Grant, Igor, and Reed, Robert, "Neuropsychology in Alcoholic Men in Their Late Thirties: One-Year Follow-Up," ***American Journal of Psychiatry 137*** 8, August 1980, pp. 928–931.
107. Adams, K., Grant, Igor, Carlin, Albert S., Reed, Robert, "Cross-Study Comparisons of Self-Reported Alcohol Consumption in Four Clinical Groups," ***American Journal of Psychiatry 138*** 4, April, 1981, pp. 445–449.
108. Begleiter, H., "Brain Dysfunction and Alcoholism: Problems and Prospects." ***Alcoholism: Clinical and Experimental Research 5,*** 2, Spring 1981, pp. 264–266.
109. Bennett A. E., Mowery G. L., Fort J. T., Brain Damage from Chronic Alcoholism: "The Diagnosis of Intermediate Stage of Alcoholic Brain Disease," ***Am J Psychiatry*** 116:705–711, 1960.
110. Berglund M., "Cerebral Dysfunction in Alcoholism Related to Mortality and Long-term Social Adjustment," ***Alcoholism: Clinical and Experimental Research,*** Vol. 9, No. 2:153–157, 1985.
111. Berglund, M., Leigonquist, H., Horlen, M., Prognostic significance and reversibility of cerebral dysfunction in alcoholics. ***J Stud Alcohol*** 38:17611769, 1977.
112. Birnbaum, Isabel M. and Parker, Elizabeth S. (eds.), ***Alcohol and Human Memory.*** Hillsdale, New Jersey, Lawrence Erlbaum Associates Publishers, 1977. Distributed by Halstead Press Division, John Wiley & Sons, Inc., New York.
113. Brandt, J., Butters, N., Ryan, C., Bayog, R., "Cognitive Loss and Recovery in Long-term Alcohol Abusers." ***Archives of General Psychiatry*** 40:435–442, 1983.
114. Cala, L. A. & Mastaglia, F. L., "Computerized Tomography in Chronic Alcoholics." ***Alcoholism: Clinical and Experimental Research 5*** 2, Spring, 1981, pp. 283–294.
115. Carlen, Peter L., Reversible Effects of Chronic Alcoholism on the Human Central Nervous System: Possible Biological Mechanisms. In ***Cerebral Deficits in Alcoholism,*** D. A. Wilkinson (ed.). Toronto, Canada, Addiction Research Foundation, 1982, pp. 107–122.
116. Coger, R. W., et. al., EEG Differences Between Male Alcoholics in Withdrawal and Those Stabilized in Treatment. In ***Currents in Alcoholism, Vol. VIII,*** M. Galanter (ed.). New York, Grune & Stratton, 1981, pp. 85–96.
117. DeSoto, Clinton B., O'Donnell, William E., Alfred, Linda J., Lopes, Cheryl E., "Symptomatology in Alcoholics at Various Stages of Abstinence," ***Alcoholism: Clinical and Experimental Research,*** Vol. 9, No. 6, Nov./Dec. 1985, pp. 505–512.
118. Eckardt, M. J., ***Alcohol and Brain Dysfunction,*** Clinical Brain Research Lab of Clinical Studies, DICBR, NIAAA, Rockville, Maryland.
119. Eckardt, M. J., Parker E. S., and Noble, E. P., "Changes in Neurophysiological Performance During Treatment for Alcoholism." ***Biol. Psychiat.*** 1979, 14:943–954.
120. Eckhardt, M., Ryback, Ralph S., Neuropsychological Concomitants of Alcoholism. In ***Currents in Alcoholism Volume VIII,*** M. Galanter (ed.). New York, Grune & Stratton, 1981, pp. 5–27.
121. Fabian, M. S., Parsons, O. A., "Differential Improvement of Cognitive Functions in Recovering Alcoholic Women." ***J Abnorm Psychol*** 92:87–95, 1983.
122. Finger, S. A., ***Recovery from Brain Damage: Research and Theory.*** New York, Plenum Press, 1978.
123. Galanter, M. et. al., Thought Disorder in Alcoholics. In ***Currents in Alcoholism Volume VII,*** M. Galanter (ed.), New York, Grune & Stratton, 1980, pp. 245–252.
124. Goldman, M. S., Reversibility of Psychological Deficits in Alcoholics: The Interaction of Aging with Alcohol. In ***Cerebral Deficits in Alcoholism,*** D. A. Wilkinson (ed.). Toronto, Canada, Addiction Research Foundation, 1982, pp. 79–105.
125. Goldman, M. S., "Cognitive Impairment in Chronic Alcoholics: Some Cause for Optimism." ***Am Psychologist*** 38:1045–1054, 1983.

126. Goldman, Mark S., "Neuropsychological Recovery in Alcoholics: Endogenous and Exogenous Processes," ***Alcoholism: Clinical and Experimental Research,*** Vol. 10, No. 2, March/April 1986.
127. Goldstein, G., Chotlos, J. W., McCarthy, R. J., and Neuringer, C., "Recovery from Gait Instability in Alcoholics," ***Journal of Studies on Alcohol,*** 29: 38–43, 1968.
128. Gorski, T. ***The Neurologically-Based Alcoholism Diagnostic System.*** Hazel Crest, Illinois, Alcoholism Systems Associates, pp. 28–31, 1979.
129. Gorski, T. and Miller M., ***Counseling for Relapse Prevention.*** Independence, Missouri, Independence Press, 1982, pp. 31–35.
130. Gorski, T. "Special Report; Diagnosing PAW Using the DSM III." Hazel Crest, Illinois, The CENAPS Corporation, January 20, 1984.
131. Grant, I. and Judd, L. L., "Neuropsychological and EEG Disturbances in Polydrug Users." ***American Journal of Psychiatry 133*** 9, September 1976, pp. 10391042.
132. Grant, I., Adams, Kenneth, Reed, Robert, "Normal Neuropsychological Abilities of Alcoholic Men in Their Late Thirties." ***American Journal of Psychiatry 136*** 10, October, 1979, pp. 1263–1269.
133. Grant, I., Adams, K., Reed, R., "Aging, Abstinence, and Medical Risk Factors in the Prediction of Neuropsychologic Deficit Among Long-Term Alcoholics." ***Archives of General Psychiatry 41*** July 1984.
134. Gregson, R. A. M., & Taylor, G. M., Prediction of relapse in men alcoholics. ***J. Stud Alcohol*** 38:17491759, 1977.
135. Harper C. B., Blumbergs P. C., "Brain Weights in Alcoholics," ***J Neorol Neurosurg Psychiatry*** 45:838–840, 1982.
136. Hartmann, Ernest L., Alcohol and Sleep Disorders. In Pattison, E. M. and Kaufman, E., ***Encyclopedic Handbook of Alcoholism.*** New York, Gardner Press, 1982, pp. 180–193.
137. Jenkins, R. L. & Parsons, O. A., Recovery of Cognitive Abilities in Male Alcoholics. In ***Currents in Alcoholism VII.*** (M. Galanter, ed.), New York, Grune & Stratton, 1980, pp. 229–237.
138. Kissin, B., Biological Investigations in Alcohol Research. In ***Research Priorities on Alcohol, Journal of Studies on Alcohol*** [Suppl], 8:146–181, November, 1979.
139. Lishman W. A., "Cerebral Disorder in Alcoholism: Syndromes of Impairment." ***Brain*** 104:1–20, 1981.
140. MacVane, J., Butters, N., Montgomery, Kathleen, Farber, Jonathan, "Cognitive Functioning in Men Social Drinkers." ***Journal of Studies on Alcohol 43*** 81–95, 1982.
141. McCrady, Barbara S. PhD., Smith, Delia E., "Implications of Cognitive Impairment for the Treatment of Alcoholism," ***Alcoholism: Clinical and Experimental Research,*** Vol. 10, No. 2, March/April 1986.
142. Milam, J. and Ketcham, K., ***Under the Influence.*** Seattle, Washington, Madrona Publishers, 1981, pp. 6670.
143. Miller, M., Gorski, T. Miller, D., ***Learning to Live Again.,*** Independence, Missouri, Independence Press, pp. 98–101, 1980.
144. Page, R. D. and Schaub, L. H., "Intellectual Functioning in Alcoholics During Six Months' Abstinence." ***Journal of Studies on Alcohol 38*** 12401246, 1977.
145. Parker, Elizabeth S., and Parker, Douglas A., Towards an Epidemiology of Cognitive Deficits Among Alcohol Consumers. In ***Cerebral Deficits in Alcoholism,*** D. D. Wilkinson (ed.). Toronto, Canada, the Addiction Research Foundation, March 1979, pp. 21–46.
146. Parsons, O. A., "Neuropsychological Deficits in Alcoholics: Facts and Fancies." ***Alcoholism: Clinical and Experimental Research,*** 1:51–56, 1977.
147. Parsons, O. A. & Leber, W. R., "The Relationship Between Cognitive Dysfunction and Brain Damage in Alcoholics: Causal, Interactive, or Epiphenomenal?" ***Alcoholism: Clinical and Experimental Research 5*** 2, Spring, 1981, pp. 326–343.
148. Pishkin, Vladmir, Lovallo, William R., Bourne, Lyle E. Jr., "Chronic Alcoholism in Males: Cognitive Deficit As a Function of Age of Onset, Age, and Duration." ***Alcoholism: Clinical and Experimental Research,*** Vol. 9, No. 5, pp. 400–405, Sept./Oct. 1985.
149. Porjesz, B. and Begleiter, H., "Human Evoked Brain Potentials and Alcohol." ***Alcoholism: Clinical and Experimental Research 5*** 2 Spring, 1981, pp. 304317.
150. Porjesz, B. and Begleiter, H., Brain Dysfunction and Alcohol. In ***The Pathogenesis of Alcoholism-Biological Factors,*** Vol. 7, B. Kissin and Begleiter (eds.). New York, Plenum Press, 1983, pp. 415–483.
151. Ryan, C., Butters, N. & Montgomery, K., "Memory Deficits in Chronic Alcoholics: Continuities Between the 'Intact' Alcoholic and the Alcoholic Korsakoff Patient." In ***Biological Effects of Alcohol,*** H. Begleiter (ed.). New York, Plenum Press, 1978, pp. 701–718.

152. Ryan, C. & Butters, N., "Further Evidence for a Continuum-of-Impairment Encompassing Male Alcoholic Korsakoff Patients and Chronic Alcoholic Men." ***Alcoholism: Clinical and Experimental Research, 4*** No. 2, April 1980.
153. Ryan C., Butters N., Cognitive Deficits in Alcoholics. In ***The Pathogenesis of Alcoholism-Biological Factors,*** Vol. 7, B. Kissin and Begleiter (eds.). New York, Plenum Press, 1983, pp. 435–438.
154. Sanchez-Craig, M. and Wilkinson, D. A., Investigation of Brain Function in Alcoholics: A Methodological Critique. In ***Cerebral Deficits in Alcoholism,*** D. D. Wilkinson (ed.). Toronto, Canada, The Addiction Research Foundation, March 1979, pp.21–46.
155. Segal, B. M., Kushnarev, V. M., Urakov, I. G., Missionzhnik, E. U., "Alcoholism and Disruption of Activity of Deep Cerebral Structures." ***Quarterly Journal of Studies on Alcohol*** 31:587–601, 1970.
156. Sellers, E. M. & Kalant, H., Alcohol Withdrawal and Delirium Tremens. In ***Encyclopedic Handbook of Alcoholism.*** New York, Gardner Press, Inc., 1982, pp. 152–153.
157. Silberstein, J. A., and Parsons, 0. A., Neuropsychological Impairment in Female Alcoholics. In ***Currents in Alcoholism VII,*** M. Galanter (ed.). New York, Grune & Stratton, 1980, pp. 481–495.
158. Small, J. Ed., ***Alcohol and Cognitive Loss,*** Special Supplement NIAAA's National Clearing House for Alcohol Information. Rockville, Maryland,
159. Tarter, R. E. & Alterman, A. I., "Neuropsychological Deficits in Alcoholics: Etiological Considerations." ***Journal of Studies on Alcohol 45*** 1, 1984, pp. 1–9.
160. Walker, D. W., et. al., "Neuroanatomical and Functional Deficits Subsequent to Chronic Ethanol Administration in Animals." ***Alcoholism: Clinical and Experimental Research 5*** 2, Spring, 1981, pp. 267–282.
161. Weiner, H., Hofer, M., & Stunkard, A. J. (eds.), ***Brain, Behavior, and Bodily Disease.*** New York, Raven Press, 1981.
162. Wellman, M., "The Late Withdrawal Symptoms of Alcohol Addiction." ***Canadian Medical Association Journal,*** 70:526–529, 1954.
163. Wilkinson, D. A. and Carlen, P. L., "Neuropsychological and Neurological Assessment of Alcoholism: Discrimination Between Groups of Alcoholics." ***Journal of Studies on Alcohol,*** 41:129–139, 1980.
164. Wilkinson, D. A. and Carlen, P. L., Relation of Neuropsychological Test Performance in Alcoholics to Brain Morphology Measured by Computed Tomography. In ***Advances in Experimental Medicine and Biology, Vol. 126, Biological Effects of Alcohol,*** H. Begleiter (ed.), 683–699, New York Plenum Press, 1980.
165. Zimberg, Sheldon, ***The Clinical Management of Alcoholism.*** New York, Brunner/Mazel Publishers, 1982, pp. 60–61.

DEVELOPMENTAL MODELS OF RECOVERY

Recovery has been conceptualized as a developmental process of repairing damage created by addictive disease, developing non-chemical coping mechanisms, changing personal identity, and developing new approaches to life and living. Initially it was believed that recovery was a "mirror image process" that simply reversed the damage that was created by the disease progression. It was later discovered that successful recovery demands not only the repair of past damage but also the development of entirely new coping skills, the development of a new personal identity and approaches to life and living. This skill acquisition is influenced by long-term toxicity that may require 6 to 18 months to stabilize. The following references review the basis of a developmental model of recovery from addictive disease.

166. Bean, M., "Alcoholics Anonymous I," ***Psychiatric Annals,*** 1975(a), 5(2), 7–61.
167. Bean, M. "Alcoholics Anonymous II," ***Psychiatric Annals,*** 1975(b), 5(3). 7–57.
168. Bean, Margaret, Clinical Implications of Models for Recovery from Alcoholism. In ***The Addictive Behaviors,*** Shaffer, Howard and Barry, Stimmel (eds.). The Haworth Press, Inc., 1984. Pp. 91–104.
169. Blane, H. T., Psychotherapeutic Approach. In ***The Biology of Alcoholism, Treatment and Rehabilitation of the Chronic Alcoholic (Vol. 5),*** B. Kissin and H. Begleiter (eds.). New York, Plenum, 1977, pp 150–160, 1977.
170. Brown, Stephanie, ***Treating the Alcoholic: A Developmental Model of Recovery.*** New York, John Wiley & Sons, 1985.
171. Forrest, Gary G., ***Intensive Psychotherapy of Alcoholism.*** Springfield, Illinois, Charles C. Thomas Publisher, 1984.
172. Gorski, Terence T., ***The Developmental Model of Recovery—A Workshop Manual.*** The CENAPS Corporation, Hazel Crest, Illinois, 1985.

173. Hazelden Foundation, Inc. ***The Caring Community Series.*** Center City, Minnesota, 1975.

No. 1: ***The New Awareness.***
No. 2: ***Identification.***
No. 3: ***Implementation.***
No. 4: ***The Crisis.***
No. 5: ***Emergency Care.***
No. 6: ***Dealing with Denial.***
No. 7: ***The New Understanding.***
No. 8: ***Winning by Losing—The Decision.***
No. 9: ***Personal Inventory & Planned Re-Entry.***
No. 10: ***Challenges to the New Way of Life.***

174. Miller, Merlene, Gorski, Terence T., and Miller, David K., ***Learning to Live Again—a Guide to Recovery from Alcoholism.*** Independence, Missouri, Independence Press, 1982, pp. 123–128.
175. Mulford, H., "Stages in the Alcoholic Process." ***Journal of Studies on Alcohol,*** 1977, 38(3), 563–583.
176. Rubinston, E., "The First Year of Abstinence: Notes on an Exploratory Study." ***Journal of Studies on Alcohol,*** 1981, 41(5), 577–582.
177. Tiebout, Harry M., "Therapeutic Mechanisms of Alcoholics Anonymous," ***American Journal of Psychiatry,*** 1947.
178. Wiseman, J. P., "Sober Comportment: Patterns and Perspectives of Alcohol Addiction." ***Journal of Studies on Alcohol,*** 1981, 42(1), 106–126.
179. Zimberg, N. E., Psychotherapy in the Treatment of Alcoholism. In ***Encyclopedic Handbook of Alcoholism,*** E. M. Pattison and E. Kaufman (eds.). New York, Gardner Press, 1982, pp. 999–1011.

AA AND RELATED SELF-HELP GROUPS

Alcoholics Anonymous (AA) and related self-help groups have been instrumental in assisting millions of people to recover from addictive disease. The books listed below are a partial listing of pertinent AA and related literature that is frequently used in self-help approaches to chemical and behavioral addictions.

180. Alcoholics Anonymous World Services, Inc., ***Alcoholics Anonymous.*** Alcoholics Anonymous World Services, Inc., 1955.
181. Alcoholics Anonymous World Services, Inc., ***Alcoholics Anonymous Come of Age.*** Alcoholics Anonymous Publishing, Inc. (now known as A.A. World Services, Inc.), 1957.
182. Alcoholics Anonymous Publishing, Inc. (now known as A.A. World Services, Inc.). ***Twelve Steps and Twelve Traditions.*** Alcoholics Anonymous Publishing, Inc. (now known as A.A. World Services, Inc.), 1957.
183. Bill B., ***Compulsive Overeater, The Basic Text for Compulsive Overeaters.*** Comp Care Publications, Minneapolis, Minnesota, 1981.
184. Emotions Anonymous International. ***Emotions Anonymous.*** Emotions Anonymous International, 1978.
185. Narcotics Anonymous World Service Office, Inc. ***Narcotics Anonymous.*** C.A.R.E.N.A. Publishing Co., 1982.
186. Maxwell, Milton A., ***The AA Experience.*** New York, McGraw-Hill Book Company, 1984.

NUTRITION

Nutrition is an important aspect of recovery. Significant numbers of persons recovering from addictive disease are malnourished. Many suffer from hypoglycemia and diabetes. It is important to have a comprehensive guideline to the role of proper nutrition in recovery.

187. Ketcham, Katherine, and L. Ann Mueller, ***Eating Right to Live Sober.*** Seattle, Washington, Madrona Publishers, 1981.
188. Milam, James, and Ketcham, Katherine, ***Under the Influence—A Guide to the Myths and Realities of Alcoholism.*** Seattle, Washington, Madrona Publishers, 1981.

THE RELAPSE PROCESS

In 1935 the relapse rate among treated alcoholics was 98%. Only 2% of the treated alcoholics managed to recover by maintaining abstinence. In the early 1970s forty to sixty percent of all treated alcoholics recovered. This dramatic improvement in recovery rates came directly from a more accurate understanding of alcoholism

(The Disease Concept) and the application of this understanding to clinical practice. The relapse rate has remained virtually unchanged since 1970. In order to bring about significant improvements in recovery rates, systematic study of patients who fail to recover must be completed. From this information a new and improved understanding of relapse needs to emerge and be applied in practice. The following references attempt to document the emergence of a new understanding of the relapse process.

189. Armor, David J., Polich, Michael, Stambul, Harriet B., ***Alcoholism and Treatment.*** New York, John Wiley & Sons, 1978.
190. Baekland, F., Lundwall, L., & Kissin, B., Methods for the Treatment of Chronic Alcoholism: A Critical Appraisal. In Gibbons, J. G., Israel, Y., Kalant, H., Popham, R. E., Schmidt, W., & Smart, R. G., ***Research Advances in Alcohol and Drug Problems.*** New York, John Wiley & Sons, 1975.
191. Crewe, Charles W., ***A Look of Relapse.*** Center City, Minnesota, Hazelden Educational Materials, 1980.
192. Donovan, Dennis M. and Chaney, Edmund F., Alcoholic Relapse Prevention and Intervention: Models and Methods. In ***Relapse Prevention—Maintenance Strategies in the Treatment of Addictive Behaviors,*** Marlatt, G. Alan and Gordon, Judith R. (eds.). New York, The Gilford Press, 1985, pp. 351–416.
193. Emrick, C. D., A review of psychologically oriented treatment of alcoholism. 1. The use and interrelationships of outcome criteria and drinking behavior following treatment. ***Quarterly Journal of Studies on Alcohol,*** 35:523–549, 1974.
194. Gorski, Terence T., ***The Dynamics of Relapse in the Alcoholic Patient.*** Harvey, Illinois, Ingalls Memorial Hospital, September 1976.
195. Gorski, Terence T. and Miller, Merlene M., ***Counseling for Relapse Prevention: The Workshop Manual.*** Hazel Crest, Illinois, Human Ecology Systems, Inc., 1979.
196. Gorski, Terence T., "Dynamics of Relapse." ***EAP Digest,*** November/December 1980.
197. Gorski, Terence T., and Miller, Merlene, ***The Phases and Warning Signs of Relapse.*** Independence, Missouri, Herald House, Independence Press, 1984.
198. Gorski, Terence T., and Miller, Merlene, ***Counseling for Relapse Prevention.*** Independence, Missouri, Herald House Publishers, 1982, pp 43–75.
199. Grimmett, John O., ***Barriers Against Recovery.*** Center City, Minnesota, Hazelden Education Materials, 1982.
200. Helzer, J. E., Robins, L. N., Taylor, J. R., Carey K., Miller, R. H., Combs-Orme, T., & Farmer, A., The Extent of Long-Term Moderate Drinking Among Alcoholics Discharged from Medical and Psychiatric Treatment Facilities, ***New England Journal of Medicine,*** Vol. 312, No. 26, 1986.
201. Hoffman, Norman S., Belille, Carol A., McKenna, Thomas, Cator 1985 Report, St. Paul, Medical Education and Research Foundation, 1985.
202. Letieri, Dan J., Sayers, Mollie A., Nelson, Jack E., ***NIAAA Treatment Handbook Series: Summaries of Alcoholism Treatment Assessment Research.*** National Institute on Alcohol Abuse and Alcoholism, Rockville, Md., 1985.
203. Marlatt, G. Alan, Relapse Prevention: Theoretical Rationale and Overview of the Model. In ***Relapse Prevention—Maintenance Strategies in the Treatment of Addictive Behaviors,*** Marlatt, G. Alan and Gordon, Judith R. (eds.). New York, The Guilford Press, 1985, pp. 3–70.
204. Pickens, R. W., Hatsukami, D. K., Spicer, J. W., & Svikis, D. S., Relapse by Alcohol Abusers, ***Alcoholism Clinical and Experimental Research,*** Vol 9, No. 3, 1985.
205. Robe, Lucy Barry, and Maxwell N. Weisman, Slips, Sobriety and the A. A. Program. In ***Relapse/Slips.*** Johnson Institute, 1983. Pp. 34–62.
206. Valles, Jorge, ***From Social Drinking to Alcoholism.*** Dallas, Texas, Tane Press, 1969. Pp. 89115.

What People Are Saying About This Book

Staying Sober *integrates the wisdom of the AA recovery program with all the research of the past few decades. It creates a road map to recovery. I believe in the concepts that are described in this book. So strong is my belief in their effectiveness, that we have implemented a comprehensive relapse prevention center at Ashley based upon this model.*

—Father Joseph C. Martin, founder of Ashley

The Book ***Staying Sober*** *clearly defines the process of relapse in the alcoholic patient. It provides long overdue and much needed information on relapse prevention. This work is highly compatible with the physical-disease model of alcoholism and contributes to our understanding of alcoholism as a primary physical disease. Since no one can predict which patients in treatment will need special help in this area, I consider it must reading for treatment staffs and all newly recovering alcoholics.*

—James Milam, Ph.D., executive director,
Milam Recovery Centers

Staying Sober *is superb. It is an excellent book for helping co-dependents and adult children of alcoholics to understand the relapse dynamic that has so affected their lives.*

—Claudia Black, Ph.D.

Staying Sober *has great implications not only for recovering people but also for counselors and other health-care professionals. Too many providers of counseling services believe that sobriety begins after the last drink and relapse occurs with the first drink. These professionals must start believing* *that relapse is a process not an act. I feel confident* ***Staying Sober*** *has done a great job in verifying that truth.*

—Frank D. Lisnow, president of National Association of Alcoholism and Drug Abuse Counselors (NAADAC)

Staying Sober *is an excellent book and recovery manual for the relapse-prone alcoholic. I feel this book makes a great contribution to the field.*

—Doug Talbott, M.D., Georgia Alcohol and Drug Associates of Smyrna, GA

As a recovering alcoholic, I have been helped by ***Staying Sober*** *to recognize and more effectively deal with my symptoms of Post Acute Withdrawal. Prior to reading this book, I would use sugar to manage PAW symptoms. This book helped me to recognize how to manage my sobriety-based symptoms constructively. As a result, I lost weight, started exercising and developed the ability to manage stress and promptly solve problems. The quality of my sobriety improved tremendously.*

—Micki Thomas, Relapse Prevention Program coordinator, Father Martin's Ashley

As a recovering alcoholic, I had many problems in my recovery that I didn't know how to cope with. The book ***Staying Sober*** *helped me to better understand the problems I was experiencing and learn how to cope with them. I found the information in this book complemented and enhanced what I was learning by using the 12-step program.*

—Robert S.

Staying Sober *does an excellent job of integrating relapse-prevention principles with the traditional disease framework of addiction. The developmental model of recovery gives an* *optimistic and growthoriented approach to recovery that is compatible with a learning model that stresses growth over time. I recommend* ***Staying Sober*** *as a practical manual for frontline counselors and recovering clients themselves.*

—G. Alan Marlatt, Director of Addictive Behaviors Research Center, University of Washington, Seattle, WA

Staying Sober *is an excellent resource for all alcoholism counselors and other health professionals who work with alcoholics and substance abusers. It thoroughly examines the various causative factors and pragmatic clinical intervention strategies for relapse prevention. This book is a significant contribution to addiction-treatment literature.*

—Gary G. Forrest, Ed., Ph.D., Psychotherapy Associates, Colorado Springs, CO

Staying Sober *is a significant work for the counseling profession. It is one of the most important contributions to solving the problem of relapse in the treatment field. It will be of benefit to anyone who desires to help recovering alcoholics and their family members. I recommend it for required study material for all alcoholism and drug-abuse counselors.*

—Tom Claunch, past president, National Association of Drug Abuse and Alcoholism Counselors (NAADAC)

I am impressed by how clearly this book develops insight into the nature not only of relapse but of addictive disease. Although primarily intended for members of the recovering community, it presents the problem of chronically relapsing patients in terms that can be recognized immediately by any counselor or therapist who works in the field.

—Maxwell N. Weisman, M.D. Baltimore, MD

ABOUT THE AUTHORS

Terence T. Gorski, M.A., is currently the president of the CENAPS® Corporation, a private training and consulting organization in Spring Hill, Florida. He has directed alcoholism treatment centers at Ingalls Memorial Hospital in Harvey, Illinois, and Illinois Central Community Hospital in Chicago. He has also served as coordinator for an employee assistance program for the Department of the Army at Fort Sheridan, Illinois. He has acted as consultant to numerous national and international alcoholism programs and is a frequent lecturer at national and state conferences.

Merlene Miller, M.A., through the CENAPS® Corporation, has developed educational programs and materials for alcoholism and drug dependence treatment centers. Combining her writing skill and her professional knowledge, she has authored numerous books on alcoholism and addictions.

Gorski and Miller are coauthors of the books *Learning to Live Again—A Guide for Recovery from Alcoholism* (with David Miller), *Family Recovery—Growing beyond Addiction, Counseling for Relapse Prevention*, and the authors of numerous training manuals, pamphlets, and articles.

TRAINING IN RELAPSE PREVENTION

Relapse prevention planning is a skill that requires training, practice, and supervision. Most agencies are not equipped to effectively train or supervise staff in these methods. Since relapse prevention planning is such a specialty, CENAPS Corporation offers professional training through workshops and inservice training. CENAPS Corporation will also open a Center for Relapse Prevention within a treatment center or private practice. If an agency opens a Center for Relapse Prevention, CENAPS Corporation will train and supervise the staff, develop patient care protocols and patient record systems, and link these systems into an applied research network.

For information contact

The CENAPS Corporation
6147 Deltona Blvd.
Spring Hill, FL 34606
(352) 596-8000